How to Discipline Your Six-to-Twelve-Year-Old...

without losing your mind

How to Discipline Your Six-to-Twelve-Year-Old...

without losing your mind

∿∿∿∿∿∿∿∿∿∿∿∿∿∿∿∿∿∿∿∿∿

JERRY L. WYCKOFF, PH.D.

BARBARA C. UNELL

Broadway Books

New York

BROADWAY

A previous edition of this book was originally published in 1991
by Doubleday. It is here reprinted by arrangement with Doubleday.

How to Discipline Your Six-to-Twelve-Year-Old. Copyright © 1991
by Jerry L. Wyckoff and Barbara C. Unell. All rights reserved.
Printed in the United States of America. No part of this book may be
reproduced or transmitted in any form or by any means, electronic or
mechanical, including photocopying, recording, or by any information
storage and retrieval system, without written permission from the
publisher. For information, address: Broadway Books, a division of
Random House, Inc., 1540 Broadway, New York, NY 10036.

Broadway Books titles may be purchased for business or promotional
use or for special sales. For information, please write to: Special Markets
Department, Random House, Inc., 1540 Broadway, New York, NY 10036.

BROADWAY BOOKS and its logo, a letter B bisected on the diagonal,
are trademarks of Broadway Books, a division of Random House, Inc.

Visit our website at www.broadwaybooks.com

Book design by Barbara M. Bachman

First Broadway Books trade paperback edition published 2001.

The Library of Congress Cataloging-in-Publication Data
has cataloged the previous edition as:
Wyckoff, Jerry, 1935–
    How to discipline your six-to-twelve-year-old . . . without losing
your mind / Jerry L. Wyckoff and Barbara C. Unell.—1st ed.
        p. cm.
    1. Discipline of children. I. Unell, Barbara C., 1951–
II. Title.
HQ770.4.W93   1991   90-34324
                                                              CIP

ISBN 0-385-26047-4

23   22   21   20   19   18   17

Acknowledgments

Many people cheered us on as we were writing this book. Some didn't even know that we were observing them as they went about their parenting business in grocery stores, shopping malls, and school open houses.

We thank all of those "anonymous" co-authors and the following friends and co-workers for their contributions to *How to Discipline Your Six-to-Twelve-Year-Old:* Elaine, Katie, Jill, and Joe Nelson; Telia Gilcrest; Jacque Blystone; Paula McNeill; Karen Vosler; Steve Thomas; Mary Lou Anderson; Britanny and Janet Flynn; Michel Sportsman, Ph.D.; Judy and Bob Handleman; Cathy and Pete Bunn; Donna Summers; Pam Pitluck; Linda and Barry Katz; Sherri and Bob Maver; Diane and David Marshall; Linda and Bob Oxler; Marianne Halleran and Bill Halleran, M.D.; Polly Runke; Debbie and Bill Gray; Gail and Don Roseman; Vicky Butcher; William Cameron, M.D.; Jeannie Sumner; Cathy and Jeff Alpert; Gloria Gale; Robert Fulghum; Janice Downey, M.D.; Barbara Peekner and the late Ray Peekner; and SuEllen Fried.

We also give thanks to the countless mothers and fathers who told us over the years of the struggles they were having in combining discipline with healthy family life, and to Robert Unell and Millie Wyckoff who accommodated our absences so we could share what we've learned in this book.

A special appreciation award goes to Beth Struck, Susan Protter, Marirose Ferrara, John Duff, Sarah F. Gold, Mary Wharton, and Maria Clark for helping make these ideas become more than just the pictures we painted in our minds of a practical, easy-to-read book about disciplining "childolescents."

Contents

∧∧∧∧∧∧∧∧∧∧∧∧∧∧∧∧∧∧∧∧∧∧∧∧∧∧∧∧∧∧∧∧∧∧∧∧∧∧∧

Preface

∿∿∿∿∿∿∿∿∿∿∿∿∿∿∿∿∿∿∿∿∿∿∿∿∿∿∿

All children present occasional discipline problems, no matter how understanding their parents are. Six-to-twelve-year-olds seem to have a different agenda from that of their parents as they experience the last stage of childhood and proceed through the half-child/half-adult world of adolescence, a stage that we call "the middle years" or "childolescence." But parents can close the gap between themselves and their middle-years children by following the practical remedies offered in this book.

Our intent is to show parents how to react to the discipline problems of normal, healthy children in calm, consistent, and effective ways—without imposing harsh punishments. We want to turn parents into "disciplined parents" who can control themselves when their children are least in control. We designed this book to be a handy reference for parents, a sort of first-aid book for handling inappropriate behavior. It recognizes the need parents have for brevity; for immediacy; and for direct, practical answers to parenting questions. The book offers advice on how to prevent inappropriate behavior from occurring and how to deal with such behavior when it does occur. There are also many example case histories here designed to illustrate how the strategies outlined in this book are applied to real problems.

This book was written out of the combined professional and parental experience of the authors. We have served collectively as teacher of developmental and child psychology; editor of parenting publications; and therapist in a school, hospital, and private practice, in addition to raising a total of four children. Our own experiences are supplemented by those of many other parents, who have contributed to this book.

Introduction

Some childhood authorities say that it is during infancy that the most care must be given to children's hearts and souls. Others are no less zealous in espousing the importance of toddlerhood.

This book deals with a forgotten stage of child development—the "childolescent" years, ages six through twelve. We contend that these are the "make it or break it" years when parents can have a critical impact on their children, helping them develop a positive spirit and a curious attitude about their expanding world.

Childolescents seem to combine the best of all childhood worlds. They are as innocent, loving, curious, inventive, and independent as they were in the preschool years. They are also as self-sufficient, logical, and skillful in talking and listening as many adolescents. This seemingly wonderful combination can be volatile at times, however, and can often lead to the most intense of conflicts with parents.

These children are also faced with many expectations—at school and at home—that they are often hard pressed to meet. When they see failure as imminent, they then go to war with this world that is, in their view, making excessive demands on them. This war manifests itself through the child's inappropriate behavior at home, at school, and in the community. What children need is not a return declaration of war from parents in the form of greater demands and punishments. They need parental nurturing in the form of unconditional love, guidance, and support.

Parents will have to make rules and set boundaries even as they allow middle-years children to grow up and away. These boundaries need to be flexible and grow as a child grows, and children need to understand the reasons for them. Middle-years children can understand the reasoning of parents in making rules, even though they may not *like* the rules or the reasons. These children can also understand that there are consequences for following the rules and for breaking them. In fact, the best learning comes from making mistakes and accepting the consequences of doing so.

Still, childolescents often challenge the rules. Verbal challenging of this kind should not only be allowed, it should be encouraged. It is only through being allowed to state his position that a child can feel empowered and develop an understanding of his world and his role in it.

Therefore, in order to manage the childolescents' behavior in a nurturing context, their parents must think of themselves as teachers because at their best, middle-years children are learners. When parents take a teaching approach to the management of childolescents, then their children have the opportunity to learn what they need to know in order to get along in the world.

But to be able to teach children in a way that they can best learn, teaching parents must first learn to discipline themselves. This self-discipline involves using understanding; tolerance; empathy; and above all, self-control, in coping with their offspring's inappropriate behavior. Parents who develop the self-control needed to become teaching parents are the best models that their children can have as they themselves learn to cope with a world that sometimes seems overwhelming.

This self-control needed to be teaching parents starts with self-acceptance. Parents must accept who they are in order to have unconditional love and acceptance of their children. This is the kind of acceptance that doesn't tell children that they must be someone else in order to be acceptable to their parents.

SELF-TALK

What a person says to herself—self-talk—governs her behavior. Therefore, when the parent of a childolescent calms herself down in times of stress by using helpful self-talk, she is more likely to follow through with reasonable and responsible actions. For example, when a parent says to herself, "I can't stand it when my child talks back!" then her level of tolerance for back talk will be greatly diminished. If, however, she says to herself, "I don't like it when my child talks back, but I can survive it," then not only will she be able to tolerate the back talk longer, but she will also be likely to plan adequate ways of changing this behavior. Self-talk, then, becomes a way of setting oneself up for success rather than failure.

How to Use This Book

∿∿∿∿∿∿∿∿∿∿∿∿∿∿∿∿∿∿∿∿∿∿∿∿∿∿∿∿∿

To use this book most efficiently, think of each *do* as a remedy for a certain behavior problem. Judge for yourself the seriousness of the problem and then begin within the mildest strategy first. That usually involves showing your child what to do and encouraging her to do it. If that doesn't work, keep trying each of the options offered until you find something that does work. A list of *don'ts* will alert you to some common traps parents fall into. Avoiding these actions will help prevent behavior problems from recurring or becoming more severe.

The remedies often include suggestions of specific things to say to your child. These words will feel more natural to some parents than to others. Change a word or two if the exact language doesn't seem to come comfortably from your mouth. Children are acutely aware of and sensitive to the feelings and subtle reactions of their parents. Make what you say and do believable to your child, and she will more readily accept your tactics.

We also urge you to study our "Developmental Milestones" chapter before trying the options listed in each chapter. By approaching behavior goals from a developmentally appropriate perspective, you will feel calmer and more confident as you "listen" to your child's behavior—the language of her feelings—instead of focusing stressfully only on her inappropriate behavior.

WHAT IS DISCIPLINE?

Discipline is not a punishment system designed to break a child's spirit and individuality. It is a teaching system that leads to orderliness and self-control.

Authoritarian parenting—demanding blind obedience from children and ruling them with punishment—produces child automatons who are controlled by the parents. Giving children the skills they need to cope with life—allowing children to take risks and practice decision-making within set boundaries—produces children who are secure and self-controlled.

This book was written in the belief that building trust and communicating positive attitudes about life are integral parts of discipline. They help a childolescent's spirit grow and thrive and prepare her for the forceful winds of adolescence which will soon face her.

In order for parents to discipline children in the ways described in this book, it is important that they maintain a sense of humor about the process of discipline. It is difficult to solve problems (and to see a child who creates problems as someone to love) when anger takes the place of humor.

Finally, this book illustrates the many ways that unconditional love can become the golden thread in the tapestry of your child's middle years, strengthening her sense of herself as a unique and valued human being.

The Do's and Don'ts of Disciplined Parenting

∧∧∧∧∧∧∧∧∧∧∧∧∧∧∧∧∧∧∧∧∧∧∧∧∧∧∧∧∧∧∧∧∧∧∧∧∧∧∧

Over the past twenty-five years, behavioral researchers have discovered how children can most effectively be taught the skills they need in order to deal with the world. One simple, overriding fact has emerged: Children must be separated from their behavior. If a child shuns doing chores, calling him "lazy" won't change his behavior. Its only effect may be to contribute to an unhealthy self-image, and it may possibly become a self-fulfilling prophecy. Parents can show their children that they love them even if they don't love the particular way that they are behaving.

When children behave inappropriately, it is probably because they have not yet learned a rule or how to follow it, or because they did not know a more appropriate way to deal with an experience.

In today's highly competitive age, problem behavior is also often seen in overstressed children who are angry and defiant because of the inappropriate expectations placed on them. If you are faced with sudden, dramatic behavior changes in your child, consider as many potential problem sources as possible—stress, depression, peer pressure, abuse, fear of failure—before assuming that your child simply does not know a certain behavior rule that you, therefore, need to teach him. In short, keep in mind that not all behavior problems can be attributed to normal developmental upheavals or the lack of knowledge about how to cope with the world.

Moreover, when problem behavior occurs, don't rely solely on what your child says or does; tap all possible sources of information before taking action or before making a final decision about what action should be taken. Contact teachers and others in his school or neighborhood to see if the behavior is noted in all quarters. *Problem behaviors* resulting from emotional disturbances will pervade all environments in which the child has to function. On the other hand, *behavior problems*—those which may reflect the making of poor choices, the lack of knowledge about a rule, or the testing of limits—will generally be confined to one or two environments, like home or school.

Teaching children appropriate behavior goals—ways to deal with their world within certain confines (boundaries and limits) using unconditional love—is called "discipline" in this book. The following "Do's and Don'ts" of disciplined parenting are based on the principles outlined above and are designed to change a child's behavior rather than change a child himself.

DECIDE THE SPECIFIC BEHAVIOR YOU WANT YOUR CHILD TO LEARN. Focus on a concrete, rather than abstract, behavior ("cleaning a room," rather than "being neat"). This tells your child what is wanted and centers the discipline on changing the child's behavior, not the child himself.

TELL YOUR CHILD EXACTLY WHAT YOU WANT HIM TO DO AND SHOW HIM HOW TO DO IT. When you establish a goal for your child— keeping his room clean, for example—give your child specific instructions on how to reach that goal. Say, "Please make your bed, put your dirty clothes in the hamper, put your

clean clothes in your drawer, and put your toys on the shelves where they belong." This also allows your child to save face if he does not know where to begin.

ENCOURAGE YOUR CHILD'S MOVEMENT TOWARD THE GOAL.

Rather than praising your child, praise his behavior. This builds his self-confidence and autonomy as he moves toward the behavior goal. Say, for example, "You made your bed so well this morning. Now, when your dirty clothes are off the floor and in the hamper, the room will be clean!" This praise is honest, focuses on what your child has accomplished, and guides him nicely toward the final steps he needs to complete in order to reach the goal. Moreover, it helps him feel good about his accomplishments and his ability to meet the final goal.

CONTINUE TO ENCOURAGE YOUR CHILD AS LONG AS HE NEEDS HELP IN REACHING THE GOAL.

By continuing to praise the steps your child is taking toward reaching the goal, you not only help learning to take place, you also remind your child that he is a competent person. In addition, praise continues to show the correct way of doing things, which keeps your child moving toward the learning goal.

AVOID POWER STRUGGLES WITH YOUR CHILD.

Childolescents are old enough to discover the extent to which their world is out of their control. This realization results in varying degrees of frustration, which may frequently bloom into outbursts of anger over who's got the "power" in certain situations.

Though they see that it may not be possible, childolescents want to try to have the same power that they see their parents having. By using Grandma's Rule (See "Discipline Dictionary"), you allow your child to have a sense of autonomy and control—some decision-making power within the boundaries you have set.

BE THERE. Parents don't need to be with their childolescents every minute of the day, but they do need to offer support, supervision, encouragement, and unconditional love in a warm atmosphere with clearly defined limits.

This emotional support is more important than physical proximity. Middle-years children look to their parents for guidance and authority. They also have the ability to ruminate, ponder, and think about the parental support they are getting, even when it is not concretely visible that their parents are giving it to them.

Just knowing that their parents are behind them—loving them no matter what their behavior—helps children grow to be giving, caring adults who are emotionally strong, compassionate, empathetic, and nurturing.

Parents must realize that they are the front line in the defense against their children's involvement in abusive behaviors, such as alcohol, drug, and tobacco (and other chemical) abuse, as well as other addictions. All the federally mandated programs, all the best ideas of curriculum specialists, all the expertise of drug/alcohol counselors have no chance of being successful at preventing substance abuse unless parents provide appropriate models at home and become actively involved in providing their children with the foundation of rules and structure within a caring, nurturing environment.

DON'T BE A HISTORIAN. Children usually know when they are doing something wrong, so reminding them afterward only serves to put the inappropriate behavior in front of them again. Tell children the goal that you want them to accomplish; avoid telling them what you don't want them to learn.

Instead of reminding your child that he shouldn't have been fighting with his brother, for example, leave the past fight to history and remind him to get along with his brother. That states the goal of "getting along" to your child and focuses you both on the goal, not on the inappropriate behavior.

TRY TO ACT SPONTANEOUSLY. If you're too intellectual about discipline, you will suffer from "analysis paralysis," and will find parenting to be a series of unrewarding struggles. Instead, try disciplining with affection, warmth, nurturing, understanding, humor, and love. You will find parenting more rewarding and you will also model the warm, compassionate approach to life that you want to pass on to your child.

What's Annoying and What's a Problem?

~~~~~~

Many of the behaviors discussed in this book are normal for this age group and are not usually considered problems unless their frequency and intensity cause the behavior to interfere in a child's life and prevent effective problem-solving.

FREQUENCY. When a behavior that is annoying or aversive is exhibited only once or twice, it is not usually considered to be a problem. However, if the behavior becomes a regular part of a child's life, it can lead to her general unhappiness, her inability to get along in the family or school setting, and her feeling that she is not a worthwhile person.

When a behavior begins to interfere with a child's ability to function in the world, then it needs to be dealt with. A child's experiencing an occasional fear, for example, is usually not a problem, but when her fear prevents her from going to school, sleeping at night, or allowing her parents out of her sight, then it has become problematic.

INTENSITY. Some behaviors of middle-years children can be tolerated in small doses, but when the intensity increases, then it needs to be managed. Some aggression is natural in middle-years children, for example, but when a child begins hurting herself or other people and things, she needs to be taught how to control her aggression.

Griping and Grounding Are Counterproductive

〰〰〰〰〰〰〰〰〰〰〰〰〰〰〰

The strategies in this book focus on what parents can do to help children grow to be responsible, emotionally healthy, self-sufficient adults. The positive building blocks (goals) of good behavior are shown rather than the negative punishers used to destroy inappropriate behavior.

Griping and grounding are counterproductive because they fail to set good behavior goals or to show children how to reach those goals.

Punishment is, by definition, something that follows a behavior and causes that behavior to stop. Harsh punishments, however, have not been proven to end bad behaviors; they just force those behaviors "underground," where parents will not see them. In addition, they create anger and resentment in children and teach them to respond in a violent and verbally abusive way.

For example, children who are humiliated, shouted at, or spanked rarely remember why they were punished. What they remember is the pain and humiliation of being hit—literally or figuratively—by a bigger, stronger parent from whom they want trust and love. In their anger, they may seek revenge for having been hurt both physically and emotionally.

Parents who punish frequently are seen by their children as less compassionate and caring than those parents who avoid punishment. Finally, punishment creates an external control for children rather than teaching them to control their own behavior. Children who have internal control are more content with themselves and their lives, are more curious and eager to learn, have better peer relationships, and are better behaved than children whose parents are punitive.

A Word About Praise

~~~~~~

In this book, praise refers to words or acts of encouragement that build a child's self-confidence and autonomy. Praise must allow children to take the credit for their own accomplishments and show them that they have the power within themselves to accept challenges and solve problems.

Praise should be given often as a way of helping your child understand what kind of behavior you expect of him, but it should also encourage your child to work for his own satisfaction, not yours. Asking, "Aren't you proud of the work you put into the math paper?" instead of saying, "I'm so proud of your A on your math paper!" tells your child that you believe in him and encourages him to believe in himself as well.

However, too much praise can lead children to place too much value on judgments of other people. To avoid this pitfall, make your praise honest and appropriate. Direct it toward your child's behavior and not your child. For example, after your child has brushed his teeth, say, "I like the way you brushed your teeth," rather than, "You're a good kid for brushing your teeth."

Developmental Milestones of Childolescence

This book deals with childolescence, the middle years that
follow preschool and precede puberty. However, because
children develop at their own individual rates, the age at
which they reach certain milestones can vary considerably.
In particular, there is a variation between boys and girls. In
general, girls are developmentally about six months ahead of
boys at about age six; and by age twelve, they are often a
year ahead.

It is important to view the middle years as a continuum of
development. For example, an average six-year-old will be
more dependent, less capable, less aware, less physically
adept, less highly motivated, and more loving and affectionate than an average twelve-year-old will be.

How do you know when your child has entered the middle
years? The beginning of this stage is marked by a child's
awareness of the viewpoint of others and how she appears in
others' eyes. This is a new view; as a preschooler, a child saw
herself at the center of the universe with all things revolving
around her. Parents may first notice their child's change in
awareness as the beginning of modesty in her.

With this new awareness of how she appears to others comes
a change, too, in a child's motivation. A childolescent becomes success-oriented and bases her view of herself on how
successful she believes she is at the tasks she sets out to accom-

plish. That is why it is so important to separate a middle-years child from her behavior.

Middle-years children also think of the world in concrete terms. Abstract thinking is only possible for fleeting moments, particularly in younger children.

Use these guidelines to educate yourself about the average stages of development during this period. Remember that your own child may vary from it, and that while these behaviors are normal, they may still require disciplined parenting.

6 TO 7 YEARS	<ul><li>Still much like a preschooler</li><li>Has wide mood swings</li><li>Curious</li><li>Eager</li><li>Careless</li><li>Forgiving</li><li>Modest</li><li>Enjoys the adventure of going to school</li></ul>
7 TO 8 YEARS	<ul><li>In a pivotal position between thinking the world does and doesn't revolve around her</li><li>Adapts her emotional response to what's socially acceptable while preserving her identity</li><li>Reasonable</li><li>Compliant</li><li>Silly</li><li>Sad</li><li>Dreamy</li><li>Egocentric</li><li>Tolerant</li><li>Teases</li><li>Self-conscious</li></ul>

- Wants to rehearse, practice, and refine skills over and over
- Friendly
- Perceptive
- Worried
- Wants control of her world
- Fearful of embarrassment
- Complains
- Sulks
- Wants reasons for having to do things
- Self-critical
- Has a high self-awareness
- Collects things
- Insightful
- Begins to compromise
- Timid
- Needs her attachment to her parents
- Brags
- Clannish
- Creative
- Hesitates before acting
- First stages of monitoring and evaluating her own behavior
- Critical year for feelings
- Busy with her inner life
- Is able to put herself in someone else's place

8 TO 9 YEARS

- More like an adult now
- Loves new ideas
- Shows off
- Peaceful
- Exuberant
- Attached to parents
- Has growing insights and wisdom
- Opinionated

- Eavesdrops
- Interested in money
- Wants to be like her parents
- Affectionate
- Demands praise
- Wants to be dependable
- Seeks independence
- Critical
- Sexist
- Has better fine motor skills
- Civilized
- Concerned about others
- Self-disciplined
- Self-confident
- Unkempt

9 TO 10 YEARS

- Outgoing
- Introspective
- Brooding
- Tense
- Forgetful
- Chipper
- Confident
- Trustworthy
- Honest
- Observant
- Conforms to friends
- Needs parents
- Returns to babyish behavior
- Anxious
- Easily discouraged
- Persistent
- Self-critical
- Loves the outdoors
- Seeks new horizons
- Sports-minded
- Generous

- Chummy
- Loves rules
- Uses bad language
- Sexist
- Collects things
- Self-motivated
- Perfects old skills

10 TO 11 YEARS

- Experiences the beginning of the end of childhood
- Impulsive
- Tearful
- Flighty
- Needs to be accepted by the group
- Emotional
- Hot-tempered
- Critical of younger children
- Interesting
- Hero-worships
- Devoted to Mom and Dad
- Sociable
- Careless
- Talkative and wordy
- Ethical
- Curious
- Proud
- Team-oriented
- Seeks glory
- Easygoing
- Interested in sex
- Sloppy
- Hungry
- Spontaneous

11 TO 12 YEARS

- Cantankerous
- Tries to separate from parents
- Fidgety

- Talkative
- Loud
- Sociable
- Silly
- Charming
- Wants to act like a teen-ager
- Moody
- Uncertain
- Self-conscious
- Awkward
- Emotional
- Excessive
- Either/or thinker
- Often uses good judgment
- Self-centered
- Loves overnights
- Loves humor
- Giving
- Imitates
- Money-oriented
- Loves being informed
- Slovenly
- Curious
- Competitive
- Critical
- Demands fairness
- Begins to realize that her parents aren't perfect
- May enter puberty (girls)

12 TO 13 YEARS

- Begins transition to adolescence
- Wide mood swings
- Independence/dependence struggles
- Begins to be logical
- Concerned with present experiences, not long-term consequences
- Involved with peers

- Begins to be clean
- Wants to be good
- Interested in boy-girl parties
- Eager to be with friends
- Craves information
- Well-acquainted with masturbation
- Abstract thinker
- Hates busywork
- Pulls away from parents
- May enter puberty (boys)

Discipline
Dictionary

∧∧∧∧∧∧∧∧∧∧∧∧∧∧∧∧∧∧∧∧∧∧∧∧∧∧∧∧∧∧∧∧∧

These terms are defined here as they are used throughout this book.

CHILDOLESCENCE. The period of time in childhood that marks the transition from the preschool years to adolescence, before the onset of puberty.

CHILDOLESCENT. A child who is between (approximately) six and twelve years of age.

CONTRACT. A contract is an agreement or understanding between two or more people and focuses on what must be done, who is to do it, when it should be finished, and what will be earned when the conditions of the contract are met.

GRANDMA'S RULE. A contractual arrangement that says, "When you have done what you are supposed to do, then you may do what you want to do." An example would be, "When you have cleaned your room, then you may go outside and play." This rule is the most basic contract that can be used with a child. It is effective because it offers appropriate reinforcers for appropriate behaviors. Never substitute the word "if" for "when." This leaves the child asking, "What if I don't do it?"

GROUNDING. The isolation of a child for a period of time so that he does not have access to any enjoyable activity. This is equivalent to jail time. Grounding may be for only a day or for up to thirty days.

HOME-SCHOOL COMMUNICATION SYSTEM.
A communication system set up between parents and teachers that is designed to inform parents of their child's behavior in school. It might consist, for example, of daily notes in which a child and his teacher evaluate the child's behavior. The notes are brought home for parents to review.

HOME TOKEN ECONOMY.
A system in which tasks (such as job chores) are assigned to, or behaviors (such as getting along) required from a child and for which payment is made in the form of tokens (play money or check marks placed beside tasks or behaviors on lists parents create). The child can then use the tokens to purchase desired privileges, such as television-viewing time or having a friend sleep over. The tokens may even be cashed in for money.

JOB CARDS.
Three-by-five-inch index cards with a job written on each card. The jobs are generally those outside the normal routine for the child and may be assigned either as consequences for inappropriate behavior or as ways for a child to earn privileges. Although jobs are being used as a negative consequence in this instance, the constructive nature of working, the satisfaction a child can experience from a job well done, and the praise he receives from his parents when he completes a job prevent doing jobs from taking on a bad connotation. (See HOME TOKEN ECONOMY.)

JOB CATEGORIES.
Jobs come in three categories: 1) Self-help—jobs that a child needs to do to keep himself going (brushing teeth, room cleaning, making bed); 2) Family—jobs that are routinely done as part of a child's expected contribution to his family (setting the table, vacuuming); and 3) Contract jobs—jobs that are done as neg-

ative consequences or as ways of earning money, as listed on JOB CARDS (scrubbing the kitchen floor, raking leaves). Jobs should always be age-appropriate.

MIDDLE YEARS. The middle years of childhood generally begin when a child enters first grade (kindergarten is generally still considered to be preschool) and ends at the onset of puberty. Because these parameters vary from child to child, delineating the ages at which they occur may be misleading. Also termed "childolescence."

NEGOTIATION. A skill that allows a child to pursue a "yes" after he has been told "no." It involves the child's making an offer in exchange for what is wanted. The offer may or may not be accepted by the parent. The negotiation sequence is as follows:

CHILD: May I have Tom over to play today?

PARENT: No.

CHILD: Can you think of anything I could do to be allowed to have him over?

PARENT: No. You boys don't listen when I ask you to play nicely and quietly.

CHILD: What if I promise we'll play quietly?

PARENT: Let's make a compromise. You may have Tom over for one hour. When I have seen that you are using that hour playing nicely this time, then we'll extend his visit next time.

PRAISE. A reward to encourage appropriate behavior goals. Praise refers to words or acts of encouragement that build a child's self-confidence and autonomy.

PRIVILEGES. Those activities that a child would choose for his own enjoyment. Examples of privileges are having a friend to play, getting to stay up past bedtime, arguing with parents, fighting with siblings, and having a preferred snack.

PROBLEM-SOLVING. A skill through which a problem is addressed by listing as many potential solutions as possible, evaluating each solution as to its potential outcome, selecting the solution with the best potential outcome, and trying the solution.

PUNISHMENT. An event that follows a behavior and causes the behavior to stop occurring and recurring.

RESTITUTIONAL WORK. Work assigned by parents to a child as a consequence for the child having done something inappropriate. Doing this work allows the child to make restitution for the behavior problem and also to feel better about himself.

RULES. The limits set by parents or others in authority. Rules should be stated in terms of the behavior that is wanted ("Get along!") rather than what is not wanted ("Don't fight!"). Rules can be spelled out in a "Rule Book," which can be consulted by anyone who needs a rule clarification.

UNCONDITIONAL LOVE. Love which is given with no "strings" attached. Unconditional love confirms the separation of a child from his behavior, so that he doesn't feel that he can only earn his parents' love through his appropriate (good) behavior. Unconditional love is love that is granted to him as he is, inappropriate (or appropriate) behavior and all.

WORK. Chores or jobs assigned to children because they are part of the family. Children need to work in a family—in the forms of doing self-help chores, family chores, or chores done for money—in order to understand that they are a valued part of the family unit.

Social

Problems

∧∧∧∧∧∧∧∧∧∧∧∧∧∧∧∧∧∧∧∧∧∧∧∧∧∧∧∧∧∧∧∧∧∧∧∧∧

Acting Shyly

("I'm too scared to ask anyone.")

〜〜〜〜〜〜〜〜〜〜〜〜〜〜〜〜〜〜〜〜〜〜〜

When your child says that she would rather die than go to the neighborhood block party, she's raising a red flag. She needs help with one of the most common temperament problems of childhood—shyness. Don't discount her fears as babyish, or call her a scaredy-cat. Teach your child how to become more assertive as you bolster her self-confidence. Roleplay with her to teach her ways to handle scary situations and familiarize her with the great unknown. Help her understand that she needn't fear getting burned by her peers in the heat of social situations.

Note: Keep in mind that how your child reacts to unfamiliar turf is largely affected by her *inborn* temperament. Studies have repeatedly shown that a shy child can be helped to become less shy, but she will always be more retiring than an extroverted, outgoing child.

There is also a difference between children who are genuinely shy and those who seem shy around adults or strangers. Children who cling to their parents, who fail to make eye contact, who maintain physical distance from others, and who rarely talk around strangers are usually shy around everyone.

PREVENTING THE PROBLEM

MODEL OUTGOING BEHAVIOR. Even if you

consider yourself shy, you may have learned certain ways of overcoming shyness. When your child sees you reaching out to others, starting conversations, making eye contact, and staying close to people, she will have an example to follow.

Tell her about situations in which you overcame your shyness to help her believe she can do so, too.

TREAT SHYNESS AS A SET OF BEHAVIORS. Consider shyness as a set of behaviors rather than as an insurmountable problem. By tackling these behaviors individually, each can be improved without overwhelming your child.

MODEL APPROPRIATE RISK-TAKING BEHAVIOR. Shyness has its roots in fears, but modeling how to take social risks can help your child put those fears in perspective. Say, "I called Mrs. Brown to ask her about the kitten she had advertised, even though I didn't know her. I felt kind of shy at first, but she was really nice."

Even when people you interact with are not nice, it is important to continue to model risk-taking. For example, say, "Mrs. Jones sounded kind of mean on the phone, and I felt kind of shy; but I talked to her even though she wasn't very pleasant. I didn't want her to control how I felt." This models the ability to handle rejection, one of the most devastating things that can happen to a shy person.

SOLVING THE PROBLEM

What to Do

REINFORCE OUTGOING BEHAVIOR. When your child makes eye contact, says hello to a friend, or answers a question with more than one word, encourage her behavior by saying, "You answered Mrs. Stone very nicely. I liked the way you said, 'It was nice to see you, Mrs. Stone.' "

PRACTICE BEING IN A SOCIAL SITUATION. When faced with a social situation that your child

may find stressful, practice what she will do. Say, "Aunt Helen will be coming tomorrow. Let's go through the things it would be nice to do when she gets here." Then practice every step, from picking Aunt Helen up at the airport and talking briefly with her to telling her good-bye.

PRACTICE ALTERNATE WAYS OF THINKING ABOUT REJECTION.

If your child is rejected by a friend (or to prepare a child for possible rejection) practice ways of coping through thinking. Say, "I'm sorry you're feeling badly about Sally being mean to you. When people seem to be mean, try thinking that they are not being mean to *you*, but they are just acting mean in general. Try thinking that you're okay, but that Sally just doesn't know that yet."

A second way to handle rejection is to use a food analogy. Say, "When people don't seem to like you, think of yourself as broccoli. You're okay; they just don't have a taste for you." This tells a child that everyone can't like everyone else, and that is okay.

TAKE ACTION IN SMALL STEPS.

Shyness is a set of behaviors that are best dealt with in small steps. When you notice that your child is not making eye contact with people, begin to praise any occurrence of her doing so. Say, "I noticed that you looked at me when I was talking to you today. I understand how uncomfortable that may be at times, but it is something people like to see in others. Keep up the good work!" This kind of praise describes the desired behavior and tells why it is important. When the small behaviors of eye contact, conversation, and physical proximity to others are reinforced, their chances of recurring are greatly improved.

ACCEPT THE SHY NATURE OF YOUR CHILD.

Because shy children are generally built to be that way, accept your child as she is. You can change shy behavior, but you may not be able to prevent her from feeling fear in social situations. Helping your child overcome the fear of rejection is essential and can best be accomplished by teaching new, nonshy behaviors.

What Not to Do

DON'T CALL YOUR CHILD SHY. If you label your child as shy, the label will communicate your expectations. Instead of telling people that your child is shy, describe her good points to others. Talk about her "acting shyly" rather than her "being shy" when you discuss her behavior with her so that you demonstrate shyness as a behavior rather than as a way of being.

DON'T PUSH YOUR CHILD INTO DIFFI-CULT SITUATIONS. If your child behaves in a shy way, she needs to be taught how to overcome her lack of self-confidence and fear of rejection. Pushing her into situations doesn't teach her how to be outgoing; and if she is ridiculed or ignored, her fear of not being accepted is realized.

DON'T PROTECT A SHY CHILD. If your child is shy, you may try to spare her the pain of social encounters. Don't protect her. Instead, teach your child the skills she needs to behave in outgoing ways and give her opportunities to practice these skills.

Becoming More Sure of Shirley

Though ten-year-old Shirley Mouber was as shy as her parents, they didn't become concerned about her inheriting this family trait until Shirley began having trouble making friends. Shirley's feeling shy was also making her afraid to go places with her mother.

One day, her mother said, "Shirley, everybody seems to believe that you are shy, but your father and I think you can learn how to be more outgoing. Would you like to work with us to try not to behave so shyly?"

"I guess so," Shirley almost whispered in her shy way.

"Well then, let's start with trying to use your strong voice when you talk. Let's try it now," Mrs. Mouber suggested.

Shirley answered again, but this time she spoke a little louder.

"That was great. I really liked your strong voice!" her mother said encouragingly.

Mr. and Mrs. Mouber set up a program of having Shirley's friends over after school and sending her to her friends' houses to play. At first, Shirley was reluctant to do any of the things that she had agreed to do. But with a lot of praise for any move she made toward more outgoing actions, she began to feel more comfortable.

Sometimes her mother had to impose some negative consequences when Shirley balked at inviting a friend over to play. She hated to force her daughter into doing something that was so uncomfortable, but she knew that it was best for her in the long run.

"I'm sorry that you didn't ask a friend to come play after school," her mother said one day. "Remember, we agreed that you would do that today. Because you chose not to follow the plan, you have also chosen to give up television for the remainder of the day," her mother stated matter-of-factly.

"But I was afraid to ask anyone! I'm too shy!" Shirley almost whispered.

"Please answer me again in your strong voice, Shirley," her mother replied.

"But I'm too shy to ask anyone," Shirley almost shouted.

"That's better," Mrs. Mouber encouraged her. "Now, I don't want to hear shyness used as an excuse. Remember, we practiced how you were going to ask a friend over and you agreed to the plan. Now, how can you ask someone over tomorrow? Let's practice again."

Shirley's teacher was also involved in the plan and used the same techniques at school as her mother did at home. She rewarded Shirley for answering questions in a strong voice and for raising her hand to volunteer information. They used a home-school communication system (see "Discipline Dictionary") to inform Mrs. Mouber of Shirley's progress in school as she worked to be less shy.

Shirley's behavior never became extremely outgoing, but she soon became more comfortable with and confident in herself and her new ability to behave in less shy ways.

Trouble with Friends

("All my friends hate me!")

~~~~~~~~~~~~~~~~~~~~~~~~~~~~~~~~~~~

Children don't always find friendship smooth sailing. They can be upset by waves of all shapes and sizes: arguments about who to sit next to on the school bus or whose house to play at after school. The waves can be related to neighborhood street wars or hurt feelings from being left out of an "in" clique. But the only sign of a real problem with friends in the middle years is if a child is upset over his inability to make and keep friends. If he truly does want help in navigating the rough social waters (and you are not simply projecting your social expectations on him by wishing, for example, that he were invited to more birthday parties), then teach your child social skills and problem-solving techniques.

Note: The number of friends a child has may range greatly. It is perfectly normal for a middle-years child to have one friend at a time, to have a group he calls his friends, or to have a new friend every day.

PREVENTING THE PROBLEM

MODEL GOOD SOCIAL SKILLS. A child who makes and keeps friends easily is usually one who has learned these skills from his parents' examples. Entertain friends in your home while your child is awake so he can be part of the fun. This will provide him with a model of adult-adult interactions that he can apply to his child-child relationships.

Good social skills can be modeled in school, too. Some schools offer social-skill training as a part of their curriculum because they understand that some children simply don't acquire these skills easily through casual observation. Social-skill training generally involves teaching children lessons in complimenting others, accepting criticism, and negotiating conflict.

MAKE OTHER CHILDREN WELCOME IN YOUR HOME. A child is more likely to invite friends over (and through this, learn how to make and keep friends) if he knows there is a warm, accepting atmosphere at home.

SOLVING THE PROBLEM

What to Do

TEACH PROBLEM-SOLVING SKILLS. A child who has learned problem-solving skills is better equipped to handle the problem of not being able to make or keep a friend. The problem of fighting with a friend could be solved in these stages: 1) What is the problem? ("My friend doesn't want to play what I want.") 2) What can be done about it? ("I could give in to my friend and do what he wants; I could fight with my friend; I could go off by myself for a while; or we could play what he wants for a while and then play what I want.") 3) Evaluate solutions. ("If I give in, I won't feel good about the outcome. If we fight, he will go home. If I go off by myself, he may go home. If we compromise, we will both get to do what we want.") 4) Make a decision. ("Let's make a deal. We'll play what you want for a while, then we can play what I want, okay?"

TEACH SOCIAL SKILLS. Children who learn to compliment others, to accept criticism gracefully, and to negotiate conflict with others will be able to make and keep friends more easily. Model these skills and teach them to your child by identifying them, role-playing how to use them, and letting your child practice them while you give him positive feedback.

REWARD YOUR CHILD FOR USING GOOD SOCIAL SKILLS. When you see your child exhibiting good social skills, praise his behavior by describing the skill that you saw. Say, "That was so nice of you to negotiate with your friend. You let him do what he wanted and you waited for your turn. I'm sure that made him feel good." This will encourage your child to use the social skill again.

WHEN PROBLEMS ARISE, PRACTICE. When your child has problems in social situations, it is important to practice social skills at a later time, not in the heat of the moment. Say, "I'm sorry you and your friend did not get along. Let's work on ways to negotiate with your friend so that you won't fight with him so easily next time that you are together." (See NEGOTIATION in the "Discipline Dictionary.")

What Not to Do

DON'T CRITICIZE FRIENDS. When you criticize your own friends as well as your child's, you are modeling how not to get along. When you accept your own friends and talk about their good points, your child is more likely to do the same with his peers.

DON'T BECOME OVERLY CONCERNED WHEN YOUR CHILD COMPLAINS ABOUT FIGHTING WITH FRIENDS. Children often get very upset when they fight with their friends and think that they will never reconcile. If you also get upset, then your child's worst fears are confirmed.

DON'T BE OVERLY SYMPATHETIC WHEN YOUR CHILD COMPLAINS ABOUT HIS FRIENDS.

If you are too sympathetic to your child, he may come to believe that he can get parental attention by describing every wrong his friends have committed against him. Instead of giving your child sympathy, walk him through problem-solving techniques so that he learns how to take care of his own problems without having to rely on you.

DON'T BECOME OVERLY INVOLVED IN YOUR CHILD'S FRIEND PROBLEMS.

If your child complains about not being invited to other children's houses, don't call other parents and ask them to invite your child to play. This only teaches your child that someone else will solve his problem. Though some friendship-making situations, such as signing children up for ball teams and clubs, are created by parents, it is a child's responsibility to find and make friends within these situations.

Likewise, if your child complains that other children are too mean to play with, avoid intervening. Allow him to come up with solutions to the problem and to take whatever action you both see as appropriate.

DON'T STAY BY YOUR CHILD TO KEEP YOUR CHILD FROM PLAYING WITH OTHERS.

If you are at a social gathering and your child refuses to play with other children, don't insist he play, but don't allow him just to hang on you, either. Say, "You have two choices: You can play with the other kids or sit quietly until we are ready to go." If he doesn't want to play, then he has chosen to be by himself. This may encourage him to try to make friends with the other children there. If he refuses both choices, then say, "If you don't think you can make a choice, then you've chosen to do jobs for me when we get home." Ignore his protests and enforce the consequences when you get home.

No Pals for Missy

Missy Ramsey came home from school complaining that her best friend had deserted her at recess. "I don't have any friends now. Nobody likes me," she moaned, beginning to cry.

Mrs. Ramsey also cried, because she felt sorry for her daughter. Why was Missy having so much trouble making and keeping friends? she asked herself. What was wrong with her eight-year-old daughter?

Later that night she explained the problem to her husband, Missy's stepfather. "Missy doesn't seem to have any friends. She's always complaining that her friends end up dumping her, and she can't figure out why. Have you noticed anything wrong with Missy?"

"She seems like a sweet and generous girl. She does expect her friends to do what she wants them to do, but I guess I thought that was the way little girls were."

The next day, Missy's mother called the teacher and talked to her about Missy's problem with friends. The teacher had the same opinion that her husband had, that Missy did have high expectations for her friends.

They discussed the problem for a few minutes longer, and then Missy's mother talked with her husband again. Together, they planned a way to help Missy in the friend-keeping department. When the complaints started again, they were ready with their plan.

"Mom, I'm so mad at Laura," Missy shared. "She said that she would play with me at recess, and then she went off with some other girls. I didn't speak to her the rest of the day. Wasn't she awful to do that?"

"Well, Missy, it sounds like you were disappointed in what happened. Does this mean you can't be friends with Laura any more?" Mrs. Ramsey asked.

"No! I hate her. She didn't do what she said she would do," Missy retorted.

"So when people don't do what we want, we should hate them?" Mrs. Ramsey questioned.

"Yes. They're mean!" Missy commented.

"Can you think of any other way you could have handled that problem today?" asked Mrs. Ramsey.

"Well . . ." Missy said thoughtfully, "I guess I could have gone with Laura to play with the others."

Mrs. Ramsey continued, "And if you had done that, how would you feel now?"

"I guess I wouldn't be so mad at Laura," Missy stated.

"What if you had told her that you didn't like what she did but you still liked her? That way you could have said that you were unhappy with her behavior, but you still liked her as a person," her mother commented.

"I guess I could have done that," Missy agreed.

"I'll tell you what. Next time a problem like this comes up, see if you can decide before you get mad whether you want to keep a friend or whether you want to get mad and feel badly. Let me know how it comes out."

A few days later, Missy bounced into the house bubbling with exuberance. "Mom, guess what? Today Heather told me that she would tell me a secret; and then when I asked what it was, she wouldn't tell me. I really got mad for a few minutes; but then I thought, 'Do I want to keep a friend or stay mad?' I decided I still liked Heather even if she didn't always do what she said she'll do. I told her I didn't like it when she promised me something but didn't do what she said, and I told her that I still liked her. We had a good time at recess, and tomorrow I'm invited to her house after school."

Missy's mother was as delighted as Missy was about how quickly Missy had learned to cope with situations in which others don't live up to her expectations—a hard skill for children her age to master.

Giving In to Bad Peer Pressure

("But, Mom! All my friends are doing it!")

∧∧∧∧∧∧∧∧∧∧∧∧∧∧∧∧∧∧∧∧∧∧∧∧∧∧∧∧∧∧∧∧∧∧∧∧∧∧∧

The term "peer pressure" can cause parents to wince with fear (What traps will this force lure their child into?). Children succumb to bad peer pressure—pressure to join in dangerous, antisocial, or just plain inappropriate activities—because they want to fit in and be accepted by a group of friends, regardless of the cost. The good news is that positive peer pressure is also alive and well. This can influence children to join in wholesome activities and conform to rules.

To encourage your child to yield to good peer pressure and resist the bad, practice decision-making with her to help her learn to make appropriate decisions. For example, let her choose what to do at her birthday party, within appropriate limits. This helps her gain experience in choosing activities with good goals that match your view of what choices are suitable for her at her age. In addition, ask your child what kind of a goal she has in mind for a certain activity. Ask her who will be at a certain party and what she will be doing there. Such discussions will help *you* make a decision about whether to permit or forbid the activity.

PREVENTING THE PROBLEM

FOSTER SELF-ACCEPTANCE. A child who accepts
and feels good about herself is least likely to be influenced by
bad peer pressure. Self-acceptance is built by encouraging a
child to be herself and by respecting her feelings or beliefs.

You help your child be herself when you praise her for what
she does, rather than for who she is. Saying, "Good work,"
when your child brings home an A on an assignment focuses
on what was done. Telling her, "Good girl," only focuses on
her as a person, and she begins to think that she is what she
does.

PRACTICE DEMOCRATIC PARENTING. A
democratic parent sets boundaries, outlines rewards for staying within them, and enforces penalties for going outside
them. Democratic parents also encourage individuality and
don't demand blind obedience. Saying, "I would like to hear
your thoughts about this," when you are discussing a curfew
or a certain item of clothing, for example, encourages individual thinking and gives your child the feeling that she is
accepted. Saying, "Shut up, and do as I say," tells your child
that her input is of no value and that *she* is also of low value.

ENCOURAGE GOAL-SETTING. Children who
have good behavioral goals, which are encouraged by their
families, are less likely to get involved with peers who demonstrate inappropriate behaviors. You can model good goal-
setting by involving your child in family chores and family
activities, as well as by telling her how valuable she is in
keeping the family household running smoothly.

Support your child's activities and become involved in
school and in the community. Focus on the process (doing
homework) instead of the end product (good grades) to help
your child recognize the effort required to reach a goal.

Not only do children need to set goals in school and home

activities, they also need to learn to set goals for leisure time. Children who claim to be bored are more likely to be influenced by bad peer pressure, because they have no appropriate structure or purpose to their activities. Help you child learn to keep in mind an array of appropriate free-time activities and praise her for choosing from the list.

SOLVING THE PROBLEM

What to Do

MONITOR THE PEER GROUP. When your child begins to drift into a peer group that seems headed for trouble, encourage her to spend time with other friends. If no other friends are available in her class or in her neighborhood, help her find other friends from athletic teams, for example. If your child insists on being with children whose behavior is inappropriate, restrict her activities to your home (where you can supervise them), or tell her that she can't be with certain children under any circumstance. Say, "I'm sorry, I can't allow you to be with Julie. I am uncomfortable with her behavior. You will have to choose someone else to be with."

Understand that your child may rebel when a favorite friend is put off limits. However, you can reward your child for choosing friends who you think behave appropriately by praising her for doing so, and allowing her to engage in activities she enjoys while her friend is with her. Say, "When you call Marci to come over, I'll take you both to the amusement park."

In the event that her rebellion continues and she claims, "I can play with anybody I want," respond by saying, "I understand how you feel; but it is important to be with people whose behavior is good so you can protect your reputation."

NETWORK WITH OTHER PARENTS. Talking
to other parents about your child's behavior gives you important information about their values and rules. This is useful in making decisions about the effect of your child's peer group. Networking in this way can also help you gather information about which children are choosing questionable behavior.

Networking can help you and other parents set general rules of conduct for all of the children in a particular group, for example, whether or not boy-girl parties or hanging out at the mall will be allowed. This will eliminate the famous chant, "Jenny gets to go!" You will *know* if Jenny can or can't, if you have already networked with other parents.

ALLOW YOUR CHILD TO SAY NO. Parents of-
ten discourage their children from saying no by not allowing them to disagree. If your child refuses to do something, allow the refusal, yet tell her what the consequences are. Say, "Yes, I understand that you don't want to clean your room today; but when you have cleaned it, then you will be free to go out and play. If you don't clean your room, you will just have to wait to go out until you decide to do what I have asked."

INSIST ON YOUR CHILD'S JOINING APPROPRIATE GROUPS AND ACTIVITIES.
When you child chooses a peer group that you believe is inappropriate, expose her to a group whose activities are appropriate in your view, such as a church youth group, a bowling league, or any other group with clearly defined goals.

Chances are good that *you* will have to sign up your child (she may see the group as "nerdy"), deliver her to the activity, and pick her up after the event. When she complains that she is miserable, say, "Yes, I understand how you feel, but you must give this activity a chance. You have two choices: You may go bowling and have a good time, or you may go and be miserable. Refusing to go is not one of your choices." Give the new group six months to a year to win your child's approval. After that, you may allow her to quit.

You may, similarly, insist on your child's participating in family activities rather than group activities with poor goals. Say, "You may go to dinner with the family and have a good time, or you may go and have a miserable time. You decide."

PRAISE YOUR CHILD'S APPROPRIATE ASSOCIATIONS.

When your child chooses an appropriate friend, praise her decision by saying, "You seem to have made a really good choice of a friend. I hope you feel good about your choice." This kind of praise is also important when your child makes good decisions to do anything that you believe is appropriate.

What Not to Do

DON'T PUT DOWN PEERS.

When you put down your child's peers, you are also putting down your child, who chose them to be her friends. This damages her self-concept and pushes her closer to the inappropriately behaved peers. If you believe that you need to make a point to your child about friendship choices, focus your remarks on her friend's problem behavior and express your empathy about it. Say, "I'm sorry that your friend, Jenny, chooses to behave like she doesn't know rules about stealing. It's too bad she believes she must steal to be liked. I wish we could help her."

DON'T OVERREACT TO PEER PROBLEMS.

Getting angry or upset about your child's choice of peer group only cements her desire to be with that group. She may see you as the enemy who is attacking her position, and the members of the peer group may become her only friends and allies. It is important to try to remain on your child's side, regardless of the inappropriate behavior. Say, "I'm sorry that you and the other girls threw rocks at Bret. It is hard not to do what the other girls are doing. Can you think of a way you could have told them you didn't want to?"

After your child has responded, say, "Now, because you did

follow the group, you must go to Bret's house and apologize to him. When you get back, let's work on ways you can make a better decision when your friends want you to do something that you know is wrong." Then, problem-solve with your child to come up with options for her to choose the next time she is confronted by bad peer pressure.

DON'T ASK "WHY" QUESTIONS. Asking your child why she is going to the mall puts her in the position of having to defend herself. Instead of asking why, say, "You're going to the mall because . . . ," and let your child answer why. Letting her finish this sentence is a more conversational and less accusatory way to elicit an answer to your question.

〜〜〜〜〜〜〜〜〜〜〜〜〜〜〜〜〜〜〜〜〜〜〜〜〜〜〜

Life in the Pressure Lane

If you knew how twelve-year-old Andy Roseman dressed, what he ate, and how he cut his hair, you would also know those things about his friends, Dave and Brad. Peer pressure was alive and well with the three boys, but Andy's parents were not concerned because their son was taking on his friends' positive traits. They didn't mind his being influenced as long as the influence was appropriate.

This happy state of affairs was disrupted when a new boy, Brandon, arrived at school. He was a little older than Andy's group, and he seemed a lot more worldly—dressing like some of the more unruly rock stars and sporting a pierced ear. His haircut was quite outlandish by the Rosemans' standards.

Because he seemed older and more powerful, the boys began to follow Brandon's lead and started to pester their parents for unusual clothing and hair styles. Odd expressions and obscenities began to spice up their language. None of the boys wanted to play with anyone else now. Andy, as well as the others, began to spend more and more afterschool time with Brandon. Andy's teacher and the parents of many of Andy's friends became concerned as they watched their boys fall under Brandon's spell. The situation became critical when the boys were caught vandalizing cars in a parking lot at a shopping center.

The first step that the Rosemans took was to begin talking with the parents of the other boys involved. This networking was the one way they knew that they could find out what was really going on with the group. They also had a series of talks with Andy.

"Andy, we would have wanted you to say no when your group of friends decided to destroy cars," Mr. Roseman began. "Because you didn't do that, we would like to teach you how to say no. When you learn to do that, then we can talk about decision-making, too."

Then they role-played saying no with Andy, asking him to try the steps that they had devised for him to use when faced with negative peer pressure.

"Andy, let's go throw rocks at cars as they pass under the bridge on the highway," Mr. Roseman said, as he took the role of one of Andy's friends.

"I like doing things with you, but I don't want to do that. It's dangerous and somebody might get hurt. Besides, we'd be busted. Let's go play some ball on the school playground instead," Andy answered as he followed the steps his parents had outlined.

"No, come on, Andy, let's go throw rocks! What are you, chicken?" his dad insisted.

"No, I can't do that. It's wrong! I'll see you around. I'm going home now," Andy answered.

"Great job, Andy," his parents praised. "Now how can you decide to say no when you need to refuse to go along with the crowd in dangerous situations?"

"I guess I'll have to think about everything first. I knew what we were doing was wrong, but everybody was doing it. I just couldn't say no," Andy said thoughtfully.

"Because it is so tempting to do what the others are doing, we are going to have to help you learn to make good decisions on your own," the Rosemans explained warmly. "Playing with your friends at our house will be allowed so that we can be around if you need us. You'll have to show us that we can trust you again. Do you understand?"

Andy decided to think before he acted and, in so doing, won more and more freedom. Because his friends' parents were all talking to each other about their boys' activities and keeping an eye on what the group was doing, even Brandon began to change his ways. He began to respond to the positive peer pressure and eventually became one of the gang again. Only this time, he imitated the other boys—becoming one of the good guys in the eyes of his peers and their parents.

Sibling Rivalry

("I don't want my brother to have more than I have!")

∧∧∧∧∧∧∧∧∧∧∧∧∧∧∧∧∧∧∧∧∧∧∧∧∧∧∧∧∧∧∧∧∧∧

The only way to avoid sibling rivalry is to have only one child. Why? Because when two or more individuals share the same space, conflict naturally ensues. Though you cannot eliminate the competition for time and attention that causes sibling rivalry, you can teach your children how to get along by focusing on the positive "getting-along" goal, instead of the negative "not-fighting" goal. With this finish line to shoot for, children can compete to win the rewards of receiving privileges instead of trying to avoid punishments.

PREVENTING THE PROBLEM

MONITOR TELEVISION-VIEWING. Comedy
programs in which putting others down is the major source of humor encourage children to deal with their siblings in the same way. Help your children interact more appropriately with each other by controlling the amount and type of television they watch.

SET GET-ALONG RULES. It is best to tell children
at a neutral time what the rules are so they know what will happen when they choose to get along or not get along. Say, "I want you children to get along. That's our family goal. When you do get along, you get to do what you want to do, within house rules. I don't care who starts a fight; you're both going to get along or work for me. You choose how you want things to be."

MODEL LOVING AND CARING FOR OTHERS.
Children who see their parents reacting in empathetic ways toward each other and toward others learn how to care about the welfare of others.

ENCOURAGE GETTING ALONG.
Say, "Thank you for getting along," or, "You are all getting along so nicely." Your children will be encouraged to get along if in doing so they reap the rewards of your praise.

CONSTRUCT ACTIVITIES THAT ARE AGE-APPROPRIATE.
Help each of your children become involved in activities suited to his interests and abilities. This reduces the chances that one or another of them will become so frustrated over not being able to play a game or sport that he will resent those who can.

SOLVING THE PROBLEM

What to Do

SET GETTING-ALONG GOALS FOR YOUR CHILDREN.
Describe to your children what you mean by "getting along," so they understand what is expected of them. Getting along must become a very important goal to them in order for them to overcome their natural tendencies to become rivals.

GIVE SQUABBLERS CHOICES.
When children are not getting along, give them the choice of continuing to squabble and being put to work, or of getting along and being able to continue to play. Assigning jobs to rule breakers as a consequence gives children the opportunity to make up for transgressions and to work toward a positive outcome. Say,

"I'm sorry you are not getting along. Remember the rule? You may either get along or you may work for me. Now, since you chose not to get along, here are your jobs."

What Not to Do

DON'T COMPARE YOUR CHILDREN WITH THEIR SIBLINGS OR OTHERS. Saying, "Why aren't you a good student like your brother?" only sets up competition between your children and creates a more intense rivalry.

DON'T BECOME A MEDIATOR IN YOUR CHILDREN'S DISPUTES. When parents intervene in disputes, each child thinks that his parent is taking sides— which only increases the rivalry.

DON'T ASK WHO STARTED IT. Trying to find out who instigated a conflict only leads children to blame each other. Assume that each child is at fault for not getting along with his sibling so that each must suffer the consequences.

DON'T LET CHILDREN FIGHT IT OUT. They only learn how to fight from this exercise. Remember, the goal is to encourage children to get along with each other.

DON'T TRY TO MAKE THINGS "FAIR." When your child says, "It's not fair that I can't go to Jack's house and Mike can," say, "I'm sorry you feel it's not fair, but because you chose to continue not to get along with your sister Mary, you cannot go to Jack's. Mike did not hit Mary, so he can go to Jack's. That is the consequence of your breaking the rules."

The Flynn Family Feuds

Jack and Jill may have been loving siblings in the nursery rhyme, but loving was not a word that Jack and Jill Flynn's mother would apply to the relationship between her children.

Twelve-year-old Jack was the eldest and, as such, believed he should rule the roost. So he teased his ten-year-old sister unmercifully, and she had become an expert at retaliating. Life in their house seemed to be a continual war.

"Stop it! Can't you two get along? You're driving me crazy!" their mother would cry. Jack and Jill would stop fighting for a while, but then they would start again.

Finally, their parents sought help in ending the war, and a plan was devised. The warring siblings were attentive when their parents outlined the new rule. "We want you to get along," their parents said. "As long as you are getting along, you may do what you want within the house rules. If you choose not to get along, then you will work for us by doing extra chores. So you both need to decide how you want it to be. Do you want to get along, or do you want to work for us?"

Both Jack and Jill readily agreed to follow the new plan; but soon, they began fighting over a television program.

"I'm sorry you aren't getting along," Mrs. Flynn noted when she heard their fighting. "Here is a job for you to do, Jack, and here's one for you, Jill. When your jobs are done, I'll inspect them and then you are free to either get along with each other or to work for me some more. You choose how you want it to be—"

"But she—" Jack interrupted, only to be interrupted by Jill who said, "But Jack started it."

"I don't want to hear about it," Mrs. Flynn said matter-of-factly. "Your job is to get along. If you can't do that, then you are going to work for me. That's the rule. Now when your jobs are done, you will be free to do what you like."

Jack and Jill did their jobs on this occasion and on several other days, as well, before they learned that fighting didn't pay. Meanwhile, they frequently heard their parents say, "Thank you for getting along," or "I like the way you two are getting along," statements which were both subtle reminders of the rule and encouragement for their children to opt to make peace, not war, with each other.

Bad Manners

("Who cares about using manners?")

~~~~~~~~~~~~~~~~~~~~~~~~~~~~~~~~~~

"Gosh, Mom! Why did you make me look like an idiot in front of all my friends?" your child squealed when you urged her to say, "Thank you," before leaving a birthday celebration. The problem with teaching middle-years children manners is that parents often do it in a negative way. They wait until they see a display of bad manners, then they correct the problem by nagging or punishing their child in public. Neither of these steps builds good self-image in a child.

Instead, enlighten your child about rules of good manners in private and at a neutral time (not in the heat of battle). Help her learn the finer points of making friends, interacting with teachers, and handling relationships in general, in a safe, accepting, loving social-skills laboratory called "family."

PREVENTING THE PROBLEM

MODEL GOOD MANNERS. A child whose parents treat her in a mannerly way is more likely to use good manners herself. Request rather than demand that your child do things, and say please and thank you to her as you would to anyone.

USE FORMAL TABLE MANNERS WHEN EATING AT HOME. Don't wait until you're in public to tell your child how she should use her napkin, fork, or knife. Those lessons are soon forgotten if they are not reinforced at the dinner table at home.

ESTABLISH RULES FOR GOOD MANNERS.
Establishing rules that govern manners tells a child when and how manners are expected. Saying, "The rule at the dinner table is . . . ," or "The rule when we greet people is . . . ," helps your child think of what is expected in particular situations.

SOLVING THE PROBLEM

What to Do

PRAISE THE USE OF GOOD MANNERS. A
child learns through praise. Statements such as, "You are holding your fork so nicely," or "Isn't it nice how you're keeping one hand in your lap while eating," not only remind a child of the expectations you have for her but also encourage her to repeat the behavior.

PRACTICE MANNERS WHEN MISTAKES ARE MADE. When you see your child eating her peas
with her fingers, help her to remember the proper way to eat by having her practice it. Say, "I'm sorry that you forgot to eat your peas with your fork. Now we must practice lifting the fork to our mouths, saying, 'I like eating with a fork.' " This consequence is so undesirable that your child will avoid making the same mistake again.

USE GOOD MANNERS AT HOME. Good manners should be modeled at every meal. If you forget to use
your manners, ask your child to remind you of the rule. Have her say, "Dad, what's the rule about elbows on the table?" When such a reminder is given by your child, thank her and correct the error.

PRAISE GOOD MANNERS. Your child is much more likely to do the things you want her to do when you praise her behavior. Praising behavior accomplishes two goals: First, it tells your child what the desired behavior is; and second, it gives her the parental attention she desires. It is important to focus praise on the behavior and not on your child. "You certainly asked nicely to have the plate passed" would be appropriate praise.

TEACH TO THE ERROR. When your child has displayed bad manners, set aside time to teach her appropriate manners. First, set the scene. Say, "When answering the telephone, the caller certainly likes to talk to someone who uses good manners." Then demonstrate the new behavior by saying, "One moment, please, I'll call her. In this case, writing the words on an index card and placing it by the telephone will help remind your child of the new skill to be used. Finally, praise the use of the new skill when you hear it. For example, call your own home when you know your child will be there, to test the system of teaching her telephone skills.

What Not to Do

DON'T NAG ABOUT MANNERS. Nagging only creates anger and resentment, and teaches a child to wait to be reminded to do what is required. Instead of nagging, ask your child about the rule and praise her following it.

DON'T COMPARE YOUR CHILD WITH ANOTHER. Saying, "Why don't you have good manners like your friend John?" will only make your child resent John without improving her manners. Children learn best when lessons are presented in positive ways.

DON'T BECOME ANGRY WHEN YOUR CHILD IS RUDE. Angrily pointing out your child's mistakes in front of others makes her feel ashamed and resentful, and doesn't teach her how to be polite. Instead, ask yourself what your child needs to learn and teach her those skills at a neutral time.

∿∿∿∿∿∿∿∿∿∿∿∿∿∿∿∿∿∿∿∿∿∿∿

Chuck, the Rude and Crude Chewer

"Mom, Ricky made fun of me when we were eating lunch," six-year-old Chuck Prater told his mother one day. "He said I ate like a pig. And when I burped out loud, his mother said that I wasn't being polite. Why don't they like me? I thought Ricky was my friend," he continued, beginning to cry.

"It's not that they don't like you, it must be that they don't like your behavior," his mother said confidently.

Chuck's parents tried nagging him about his bad table manners. At dinner, there was a constant barrage of, "Sit up straight" and "Chew with your mouth closed." But these remarks only caused Chuck to feel nervous and eventually angry and rebellious.

It was then that his dad hit on an idea. He had spent some of his time in performance appraisal on his job and he knew the principles that were effective in changing behavior. First, both he and his wife had to make sure that Chuck knew how to do what was required of him. Then, every time that he was exhibiting an appropriate behavior, the behavior needed to be pointed out. If problems remained, his parents decided, then they could conduct some training sessions with him.

That night at dinner, Chuck's parents announced their first target behavior. "Your mom and I want to be sure that you can hold your fork properly, Chuck," his father explained. "You hold it just like you hold a pencil at your plate. Please pick it up and put it in your hand as if you were going to write."

When Chuck did as he was told, his father said, "That's good. Now take the pencil out and put the fork in its place just like you were going to write with the fork. Now you can eat with your fork in a proper way," Chuck's dad stated, with noticeable pride.

For the next few nights, his parents put a pencil and a fork at Chuck's place. When he was using his fork correctly, one of his parents would say, "You are holding your fork properly tonight!"

Chuck would beam and try to remember the proper way to hold it. When he made a mistake, he was required to hold the pencil and then replace it with a fork.

As soon as Chuck had mastered each skill, a new one was introduced in the same way as the fork skill had been. Soon Chuck had a full set of manners and a new sense of confidence, both of which he could use when visiting his friends' homes.

Stepping Over Sexual Boundaries

("I only wanted to know what she looked like. I didn't do anything wrong!")

∿∿∿∿∿∿∿∿∿∿∿∿∿∿∿∿∿∿∿∿∿∿∿∿∿

If you catch your six-to-twelve-year-old exploring his own body or those of his peers, should you blow the whistle? The sexual curiosity of middle-years children is a healthy characteristic of childolescence. And since it generally manifests itself as harmless behavior, treat it as such, within certain limits. Satisfy your child's desire to understand his emerging sexuality by helping him learn that his sexual feelings are natural. At the same time, teach him that there are appropriate and inappropriate times and places for sexual exploration and information about sexuality.

PREVENTING THE PROBLEM

ANSWER YOUR CHILD'S QUESTIONS DIRECTLY. When your child asks questions or shows an interest in sexuality issues, talk as openly and comfortably as possible. Don't worry about giving your child too much information. He will take in what he can understand and store the remainder until later, when he is developmentally ready to understand it. A child can't have too much information; but with too little, he will fill in the blanks with what often turns out to be false information.

If you are uncomfortable with giving sexual information to

your child, ask his health practitioner about books and sex education classes that are recommended for bringing up the subject with a middle-years child.

MODEL APPROPRIATE SEXUALITY. Parents who show love and caring (physically and emotionally) for each other are modeling appropriate sexual interaction. Your child learns from you how to be loving and caring in ways that are not openly sexual, so that the most important lessons in sexuality are centered around love and respect. Displays of kissing, hugging, and caressing between parents who love each other show children an appropriate physical view of love. Giving a child the same love and respect that you give to your spouse can also make a child feel good about his own sexuality.

SHOW YOUR CHILD HOW TO FIND AN-SWERS TO HIS QUESTIONS. When your child has questions, show him how to find answers to those questions through resource materials that are available in your home or local library. His knowing how to find appropriate answers to his questions can help him avoid inappropriate explorations with other children or being embarrassed when talking to adults about sexuality.

ENCOURAGE PRIVACY. Encourage the concept of privacy as it relates to your child's body, in a variety of areas (such as toileting, bathing, and dressing). Respecting privacy in these areas helps children understand and respect the privacy of adults and the fact that some things done in private are not done in public.

SOLVING THE PROBLEM

What to Do

SET RULES FOR SEXUAL EXPLORATION.
When you discover your child in the process of trying to satisfy his sexual curiosity, teach him the rules for doing so appropriately. Say, "When you want to know the answers to questions you have about your sexuality, please come to me so I may answer your questions. If I don't know the answer, I will find it." This helps establish a precedent for your child's seeking answers to these issues (and others) in an appropriate way.

EXPLAIN THAT SEXUAL EXPLORATION MAY UPSET SOME PEOPLE.
When you see your child and another in mutual exploration of their bodies, say, "Looking at others' bodies is one way of finding out how they look, but some people may not believe that it is appropriate for you to be doing that. Instead, please come to me when you are curious, and we will try to find the answers to your questions together."

NETWORK WITH OTHER PARENTS.
If you discover your child engaging in sexual exploration with other children, don't overreact to this circumstance. First talk with the parents of the other young people to plan a unified approach in responding to this situation. By having the support of your peers, you may feel more confident about satisfying your child's natural curiosity through sex education. Your doing so will encourage him to avoid seeking clandestine ways to gain information.

What Not to Do

DON'T HIDE THE FACTS. When you hide the truth about the facts of life from your child, he will fill in the details with his imagination; his fantasizing often leads him to engage in inappropriate activities simply because he wants to make his fantasy become reality. An additional reason to tell your child the truth about sexual matters is the obvious one—lying about *anything* ultimately teaches him that you are dishonest.

DON'T OVERREACT. Your overreaction to sexual exploration (by shouting at him or spanking him, for example) can teach your child that his sexual curiosity is evil and must be hidden from adults in order to avoid punishment for it. Because sexuality is a natural phenomenon, treat sexual curiosity as a natural part of a child's life so that he can grow up with a healthy attitude about it.

$\wedge\!\wedge$

Is It Sex Yet?

Nine-year-old Alan Robinson was notorious for wanting to know how everything worked. He had always been curious; so when he wanted to know about sex, it seemed perfectly reasonable for him to go ask his parents, just as he went to them with all of his other questions. However, his parents found that they were too embarrassed to talk about sexuality issues with their child.

So Alan took his questions to his friends. His nine-year-old companions supplied him with a lot of superstition and falsehoods, which confused him even more. In the absence of good information, Alan began to seek answers in other corners of his world.

Mrs. Robinson became painfully aware of Alan's continuing hunger for information about sex when their neighbor, Mrs. Kaufman, called, crying and screaming. After calming her down, Mrs. Robinson learned that Alan and his friend, Joe, had talked Sara Kaufman into going with them to their garage, and they had all stripped off their clothes. It was in this naked state that Mrs. Kaufman had discovered them. They were busy exploring each other's bodies as they attempted to figure out what sex was all about.

"But we weren't doing anything!" Alan cried as Mrs. Robinson banished Alan to his room for the day. Still, she believed that this punishment would not solve the problem. So when Mr. Robinson came home that night, his wife and he held a serious conference.

"There's a sex educator named Mrs. Arnold at church. Maybe we should call her to see what we should do," Mr. Robinson suggested.

Mrs. Arnold assured the Robinsons that Alan's curiosity was natural, and that there was no need for them to be embarrassed about it. The Robinsons decided that what Alan needed most of all was sex education. Mrs. Arnold gave them some books that pointed out the importance of the family in the education process and how, when children learn about sexuality in the security of their home, they can avoid believing rumors or exploring inappropriate ways to get the knowledge they are seeking.

Embarrassed as they were by the subject, the Robinsons began Alan's lessons. They forced themselves to be as open and honest as possible as they showed their son the pictures in the book. At first Alan was reluctant to ask any questions, but after a while, he felt more comfortable and the questions flowed.

"But how do babies really get into the mother's stomach? You mean semen actually comes out of the man's penis? When the egg dies because it's not fertilized, blood and stuff comes out of the woman's vagina? That's gross!" Alan exclaimed.

The Robinsons answered Alan's questions directly, talked about respecting the privacy of others, and made special points about the importance of his talking to *them* about sexuality issues in order to get correct information before participating in sexual relations.

Mr. and Mrs. Robinson tried hard to model respect for each other and for Alan, as well. They realized that learning about his sexuality was a very important and natural part of their child's healthy growth and development.

Lying

("I can't tell the truth!")

〰〰〰〰〰〰〰〰〰〰〰〰〰〰〰〰〰〰〰〰〰

The childolescent who spins alibis to keep from getting into trouble or proclaims "I did it!" when she's asked if she cleaned up her room (and she didn't do it) lies because she believes that she cannot cope with the demands that are made on her. She lies to avoid punishment because she doesn't believe she can stand the consequences of her wrongdoing; she lies to avoid responsibility because she doesn't think she can bear to do what's necessary; and she lies to make herself look better because she doesn't think she can tolerate being *only* herself.

Help your child choose to cope by demonstrating that you love her as she is—without the embellishments of untruths. The consequences for lying must help your child understand how lying destroys trust. In addition, you need to help your child feel good about herself, though not about what she did. Then your child will increase her self-confidence so that she can cope with the world as herself, not the Superself she wishes she was.

Note: There is a difference between lying and fantasizing. Be sure of the intent behind your child's misleading statements—distinguish between deliberate attempts to deceive and stories that are made up as she tries to differentiate where the real world stops and her imagination begins.

PREVENTING THE PROBLEM

ENCOURAGE YOUR CHILD TO TELL THE TRUTH. Teach your child about the rewards of behaving

honestly by rewarding her when she does. The reward children like best is praise from parents. Say, "I like it when you tell the truth. Thanks for telling me the truth."

MODEL TELLING THE TRUTH. It is difficult for your child to understand the importance of honesty if you lie to her (and others). Children of all ages need to hear the truth from their parents, no matter how difficult it may be to swallow, in language that is appropriate for their age.

TO ENSURE THE TRUTH, CHECK THE STORY. Rather than asking your child whether her homework is finished, simply ask to see it. This tells your child that you will be checking her work, encourages her to complete it, and prevents her from lying about it just to avoid a consequence.

GIVE EXAMPLES. Teach your child the benefits of telling the truth by using examples from real life in which telling the truth, not lying, helped people cope with their predicaments.

SOLVING THE PROBLEM

What to Do

REACT CALMLY WHEN YOUR CHILD IS CAUGHT LYING. Overreacting will encourage your child to continue to lie in order to avoid your wrath.

A CHILD WHO LIES SHOULD MAKE RESTITUTION. Give your child jobs to do when she is caught lying, so that she can make restitution for her wrongdoing. In this way, you allow her to feel good about the outcome of

the conflict and to feel okay about herself if not about what she did.

PRACTICE TELLING THE TRUTH. When your child lies to you, say to her, "Let's see how telling the truth sounds. Please say, 'Yes, Mom, I was throwing the ball at the house and broke the window.' " After your child tells the truth, then calmly instruct her in the ways she can make restitution for her wrongdoing by buying a new pane of glass and helping to install it, for example.

What Not to Do

DON'T CONDEMN YOUR CHILD FOR THE LIE. A child who is labeled "liar" stands a better chance of fulfilling the label—believing that what she does is what she is. Remember to separate a child from her behavior to enhance her ability to feel okay about herself, even though you (or she) might not like what she did.

DON'T ASK QUESTIONS. Don't ask questions to which you already know the answer. Children will lie to take a chance that they won't get caught.

DON'T TAKE LIES AS PERSONAL ATTACKS. Children don't lie in order to show a parent disrespect. They lie in order to save face while testing what your reaction will be.

⌇⌇⌇⌇⌇⌇⌇⌇⌇⌇⌇⌇⌇⌇⌇⌇⌇⌇⌇⌇⌇⌇⌇⌇⌇

The Truth About Amy

"Liar, liar, pants on fire!" the children shouted at eight-year-old Amy Krigel after she told another of the tall tales for which she was so famous. She knew as well as everyone else that her stories were made up to make her look better than she thought she was. But Amy had been lying for such a long time that it was even getting hard for her to know the difference between a lie and the truth.

Not only did Amy lie about her accomplishments, but when backed into a corner, she would skillfully lie her way out. One morning, Mrs. Krigel had asked her whether she had finished her homework the night before; Any had assured her that it was all done.

"Let me see it!" Mrs. Krigel had insisted, but Amy had convinced her that it would be too much trouble getting it out of her backpack and that she wouldn't understand the assignment anyway.

When Mrs. Krigel learned that her daughter's lying about her homework was beginning to be reflected in poor grades, she finally decided to help Amy learn to tell the truth, not taking Amy's stories at face value. When Amy bragged about hitting a home run on the playground, for example, Mrs. Krigel would call Amy's teacher to confirm the details. Afterward, Mrs. Krigel would let Amy know that she had done so and that she intended to verify Amy's statements until she learned to tell the truth.

Second, she decided that she would not ask questions that would allow her daughter to lie. The next time that she asked to see Amy's completed homework, and Amy started to say, "But . . . ," she cut her off. "Amy, I asked to see your homework. Now please go get it and show it to me!" she stated.

When Amy learned that she couldn't get away with lying at home, she began to tell the truth. One day, she said, "I didn't really do my chores yet," when her mother asked about her doing them. Mrs. Krigel promptly praised her truthfulness and rewarded her for being honest.

"Amy, thank you for telling me the truth," she exclaimed. "It must feel good to be so honest. Because you told the truth, I will withhold the consequences that you would have received for not doing your chores when you were supposed to But you still have to do them, and I want them done before you do anything else."

Amy vowed to continue being honest. She even began to like her new truthful self and decided that she didn't need to tell stories to make herself look better. Finally accepting herself as she was felt great.

Annoying Habits

("I've tried, but I can't stop biting my fingernails!")

∿∿∿∿∿∿∿∿∿∿∿∿∿∿∿∿∿∿∿∿∿∿∿∿∿∿∿∿∿

Popping knuckles, tapping toes, and spitting like a baseball player—bad habits such as these are usually not premeditated. In fact, the offender is typically not even aware that he is committing the crime. The habit just becomes part of his behavior, particularly in times of stress or during an idle moment. To help an annoying habit become history, minimize the attention you pay to your child's nerve-racking behavior, whether it's bouncing his knee or sucking his thumb. By making the rewards of *breaking* the habit greater than the rewards for *continuing* it, you will soon see your child's self-control skills skyrocket as you help him develop a good habit—feeling that he's a capable kid!

PREVENTING THE PROBLEM

NIP IT IN THE BUD. When an annoying, new behavior appears, do something to change the behavior before it becomes a habit. The longer it is left alone, the harder it will be to eliminate it.

MONITOR YOUR OWN HABITS. Model behavior that is free of annoying habits. If you crack your knuckles or belch loudly at the table, it will be difficult for your child to understand why he can't do the same thing.

SOLVING THE PROBLEM

What to Do

MAKE A RULE. Make a rule about when and where a bad habit may be practiced. Say, "You may crack your knuckles only when you are alone in your room. We want you to learn how to do something else with your hands. If they are causing problems, perhaps you could sit on them." This not only tells your child what is acceptable and what is not, but it gives him suggestions of ways to solve the problem. These limits also raise the cost of bad habits. Your child won't want to go to his room and sit there alone to crack his knuckles. He will generally want to be with others or where the action is.

REINFORCE THE ABSENCE OF THE HABIT.
A child needs to know when he is doing what is acceptable. If you only talk about the bad habit, then the habit gets all the attention. Instead, reinforce other behaviors that can replace the bad habit. Say to your child, "Look! You are sitting on your hands, that's great!"

WEAR THE HABIT OUT. Habits can be broken by being worn out. Instruct your child to do the habit for a set length of time. When you see your child spitting, for example, simply tell him to spit for five minutes. Soon, the lack of attention and low satisfaction level that your child receives for practicing his habit will help it lose its appeal.

IGNORE A HARMLESS ANNOYING HABIT.
If an annoying habit is ignored, sometimes it will fade out without any parental interference. In order to ignore a harmless habit, leave your child alone or think about other things when the habit is present.

ACCEPT YOUR CHILD—HABITS AND ALL.

Your child's bad habits are reinforced when you become upset over them. On the other hand, when you accept your child and his bad habits, you avoid focusing attention on the habits and avoid giving your child the impression that he is not acceptable because of them.

What Not to Do

DON'T CALL ATTENTION TO THE HABIT.

When you say, "Don't do that," in response to your child's foot-tapping, for example, your child is getting attention for doing what you don't want done. Point out instead behaviors that are the opposite of the habit. Saying, "Thank you for keeping your feet flat on the floor," can be the alternative to saying, "Stop tapping your foot."

∧∧∧∧∧∧∧∧∧∧∧∧∧∧∧∧∧∧∧∧∧∧∧∧∧∧∧∧∧

The Knuckle Crunch

Whenever eight-year-old Ronnie Fink popped his knuckles, his father would go crazy. "Would you stop popping your knuckles!" Mr. Fink would yell. Ronnie felt bad that he was annoying his father so much, but his habit had gotten out of his control.

Not only did Ronnie Fink have a habit of knuckle-popping, but he also had an irritating bubble gum-chewing habit. Often he would become so absorbed in what he was reading that he would begin smacking and slurping as he enjoyed his gum. Then he would blow huge bubbles, which would often pop all over his face.

Completely disgusted, Ronnie's father would yell at him to quit his gum-chewing habit and would make him throw his gum away. Again, Ronnie was sorry that his habit was so disturbing to his father; Ronnie's father also was troubled by his yelling at his son.

So Mr. Fink decided to take a different approach. "Sit down, son," he began. "I know that I've been yelling at you about some of your habits, and I'm sorry. Instead of yelling, I would like to make a contract with you."

Ronnie squirmed uncomfortably and started to crack his knuckles. He popped one, realized what he was doing, and promptly sat on his hands.

"That's good, Ronnie. Sitting on your hands is a good idea. That way you can't pop your knuckles," Ronnie's father praised.

"Now, let's talk contract. I'm going to keep track of the number of times you crack your knuckles. I'll do this for a week. Then I will pay you with points for each day you reduce the number below the day before. Understand?"

"I think so. You mean that if I pop my knuckles twenty times today, I get paid points if I only pop them nineteen times tomorrow?"

"That's right, Ronnie. Not only do you get paid for reducing the number from the day before, but you also get paid by the number of times that you reduce that number. If you drop three below the day before, you will get three times three points, for example. Now let's talk about what you can do with the points. Here is a list of things that you can purchase with them."

On the list were all the things that Ronnie really liked to do. If he wanted to do any of them, Ronnie realized that he would have to work for the points.

From that day on, Ronnie worked hard at keeping track of his habit, spending a lot of time sitting on his hands. Soon, however, he forgot about cracking his knuckles. It wasn't long before Ronnie no longer had to contract with his parents for points because his knuckles were out of use, as was his father's bellowing parenting tactics.

Taking Others' Belongings— Stealing

("If I want it, I'll take it!")

~~~~~~

Yesterday, your eight-year-old daughter took a pack of bubble gum from the drugstore shelf—without paying for it first. Today, she "stole" a nickel from the kitchen counter at home. Instead of calling her a thief, protect your child's sense of self-worth by teaching her how to get something she wants appropriately. In addition, help her to learn how to exercise self-control while waiting for what she wants by setting up rules about what can and can't be taken—from your home and from public places—without first asking permission to do so.

Third, establish ways your child can work to attain what she wants. In this way, she can get a taste of how to earn and spend money to satisfy her appetite for possessions.

PREVENTING THE PROBLEM

BUILD YOUR CHILD'S FRUSTRATION TOLERANCE BY RESISTING HER EVERY DEMAND.
A child who gets what she wants every time she asks will have a greater tendency to expect instant gratification.

ENCOURAGE YOUR CHILD TO KEEP HER POSSESSIONS PROTECTED FROM POSSIBLE THEFT.
When she thinks about her unattended bicycle as a potential target for theft, your child will gain a greater understanding of what it means to be responsible for her possessions. This kind of thinking encourages her to be more empathetic toward other people's possessions, as well.

ALLOW YOUR CHILD TO HAVE POSSESSIONS OF HER OWN.
Your child will more readily understand the concept of possessions if you allow her to have sole ownership of at least a few things. These things can still be shared, but they should be considered your child's own property.

EXPLAIN THE DIFFERENCE BETWEEN BORROWING, LOANING, AND SIMPLY TAKING SOMETHING FROM SOMEONE WHO "WOULDN'T NOTICE."
Discuss the meaning of the words "shoplifting," "borrowing," and "stealing" with your child to ensure that she knows the difference between taking something that she is entitled to take and something that's in a store.

GIVE YOUR CHILD THE CHANCE TO EARN MONEY SO SHE CAN LEARN THE LEGAL WAYS OF GETTING WHAT SHE WANTS.
(See CONTRACT JOBS under JOB CATEGORIES in the "Discipline Dictionary.")

SOLVING THE PROBLEM

What to Do

SET UP A RULE ABOUT POSSESSIONS.
When your child is caught stealing, enter a rule about steal-

ing as part in your House Rule Book (See RULES in the "Discipline Dictionary.") Say, "The rule is: You may have in your possession only those things that belong to you. When you want something that belongs to someone else you must first ask the person if you may have it or use it." It is important, then, to know what possessions belong to your child, so that it can easily be determined when she "mysteriously" has things belonging to others.

ASSIGN WORK TO MAKE RESTITUTION FOR YOUR CHILD'S WRONGDOING. Say,

"John, I'm sorry you chose to have your friend, Suzi's, property. You know the rule: You may have in your possession only those things that belong to you. Now you will have to return Suzi's pen, and then you will have to do some jobs to make up for breaking the rule. The jobs are scrubbing the kitchen floor and cleaning out the garage. Now, let's go take the pen back to Suzi." If your child replies, "Make me," don't get angry, just offer him choices. Say, "You may do what I asked or lose the privileges of doing what you want to do. You decide." Then follow through with the enforcement of the consequences of whatever choice your child makes.

TREAT THE PROBLEM OF STEALING AS AN ERROR THAT YOUR CHILD CAN CORRECT.

If your child thinks of herself as a thief, she is free to continue behaving as if she is inherently bad. Separate your child from her behavior. Say, "I would like to know the reasons for your mistake so I can help you not make the same mistake in the future." If your child answers, "I don't know the reason," then respond, "Let's think about it. What were some thoughts you had when you saw the thing that you wanted?"

Through discussing her reasons for stealing with you, your child is more likely to get in the habit of thinking about her behavior *before* a problem arises. She will learn that you are really on her side, helping her to delay her wants and desires until she can satisfy them appropriately.

If your child refuses to talk about the theft, don't beg or threaten her to do so. Instead, say, "I understand that you don't want to talk about it, but it is important. Here are your choices. We can talk about it and then you can do what you like, or we can wait here until you are ready. You choose how you want to handle this situation."

PROBLEM-SOLVE WHAT YOUR CHILD COULD HAVE DONE OTHER THAN STEAL.
Use good problem-solving strategies when you discover your child has been stealing. First, ask her to identify the problem. Say, "What were you thinking when you stole the candy?" Then, together, generate as many potential solutions as possible for your child to get candy without breaking the law. Finally, pick a solution with the best potential outcome.

SET UP BORROWING RULES. Children like to borrow things that don't belong to them, like their mother's good scissors, their dad's drill, or their brother's bike. Set up a borrowing rule. Say, "You must ask permission before you borrow something. Failing to do so will result in being assigned two jobs to make up for breaking the borrowing rule."

What Not to Do

DON'T OVERREACT TO THEFT. Put the problem in perspective by understanding that every child may steal from time to time and that it isn't the end of the world if yours does, too. Remember that her occasional episodes of stealing do not make your child a thief.

DON'T LABEL YOUR CHILD AS "BAD." The problem of stealing is one of behavior, not of character. View stealing as a behavior problem that can be corrected, and treat it as an error.

To Catch a Thief

"Stan the Stealer," is what Stan Wharton's brother and sister called him because he was always taking their things without asking. Several times the six-year-old had even been caught taking candy and small toys from the drugstore when his mother took him shopping. As they grew increasingly tired of trying to find things he had "borrowed," Stan's parents decided to talk to him about the situation.

"Stan, we have a problem," Mr. Wharton began. "You seem to be making the mistake of taking things that don't belong to you quite often these days, and we are all getting upset by your behavior. I don't want you to have a reputation as a thief, so I'm going to help you stop making the mistake of taking things that don't belong to you."

Stan was very upset by his father's seriousness. He knew that he took things that belonged to others, but he didn't think he could help himself. He wanted things, so he took them.

"First," his father continued, "we will make a rule: If you have something in your possession that does not belong to you, then you will have to take it back and do jobs until you have made up for taking the item. If you take something from one of us in the family, you will have to do our chores for us to make up for taking our things. Any questions so far?"

Stan shook his head. He understood what his dad was saying because he had done chores before to make up for doing things that were wrong.

"Now, to help you resist temptation, here's what I want you to do. When you see something you want so badly that you want to take it, yell inside your head, 'Stop it!' and come to your mother or me. Tell us what you would like to have, and we will help you figure out a way you might be able to get it."

"You mean I can have anything I want just for asking?" Stan asked incredulously.

"Not just for asking," Mrs. Wharton quickly answered. "Everything has a price. You will have to earn what you want. That's what we all have to do when we want things."

From that day on, Mr. and Mrs. Wharton kept close tabs on the things Stan played with and wore. He occasionally had to work for his brother or sister because he took their belongings, but soon he got in the habit of going to them to ask for something. He also began to realize that the cost of stealing was too high. He learned that he could often do without items he wanted or find an appropriate way to get them.

Inappropriate Use of Humor

("Did you see Jeff's underwear showing today? It cracked me up.")

∿∿∿∿∿∿∿∿∿∿∿∿∿∿∿∿∿∿∿∿∿∿∿∿∿∿∿∿∿∿∿∿

When a child is about nine, humor suddenly rears its hilarious head. Your child starts to lapse into giggles over riddles, knock-knock jokes, and words such as "underwear" and "bathroom." Why? Because this is when a child begins to understand double meanings in words. He also begins to understand that laughter can help him cover up his feelings of embarrassment about words; places; and most of all, people's bodily functions. Teach your child that humor can be hurtful as well as delightful by establishing humor rules—clear guidelines about what will and will not be considered funny in your household. Make sure that the cost of his breaking the rules is offset by the rewards he receives when his humor is displayed at socially acceptable times and places.

PREVENTING THE PROBLEM

PROVIDE APPROPRIATE EXAMPLES OF HUMOR. Children who are exposed to appropriate forms of humor are more likely to mimic them and will tend to adopt those forms of humor as their own.

REWARD YOUR CHILD'S SENSE OF HUMOR. Humor can help children through the most difficult

of times; so when you see appropriate forms of humor being expressed by your child, praise that behavior.

SET HUMOR GUIDELINES. Form humor rules to let your child know what will and won't be accepted. Saying, "The rule is: We speak kindly of others," can establish guidelines about put-down humor.

MONITOR TELEVISION PROGRAMS. Much of children's humor today is influenced by television. Outlaw programs that use put-downs or insults as forms of humor, pointing out why they are inappropriate. Say, "Isn't it too bad people have to talk like that on these programs? Because we don't do things like that in our family, we shouldn't continue watching those programs."

SOLVING THE PROBLEM

What to Do

IGNORE INAPPROPRIATE HUMOR. When your child begins to giggle about things you don't think are appropriate, ignore his behavior. If your child sees that these jokes don't get a reaction, he may look for others that will.

WEAR OUT WORDS. When your child frequently uses an inappropriate word as a form of humor, instruct him to say the word as fast and as loud as he can for five minutes. Say to your child, "I see that you like the word 'fart.' Because you like it so much, I want you to sit here and say it as loud and as fast as you can. When you have said the word until the timer rings, you may go out to play." Then set a timer for five minutes. Wearing out a word can make a child so tired of it that he won't want to hear it or use it again.

PUT PENALTIES ON USING INAPPROPRI-ATE HUMOR.
When a child makes fun of others, the consequence should be making up for being unkind. Assign your child jobs to do as a way for him to make restitution. Say, "I'm sorry you chose to make fun of Bobby. When you have apologized to Bobby, then you will do a job for me to make up for that unkindness." Assigning jobs to make up for any inappropriate behavior teaches that doing something constructive can make up for doing something inappropriate, and the completion of a job gives a child a sense of self-satisfaction which can enhance his self-image.

What Not to Do

DON'T REINFORCE INAPPROPRIATE HU-MOR.
Keep a straight face when something inappropriately funny has been said to avoid paying off that kind of humor.

DON'T BECOME UPSET OVER BAD HU-MOR.
Often a child says shocking things because they sound funny to him. If you overreact, the humor may be gone, but the shock value remains, increasing the chances your child will use the bad humor again just to get your attention.

DON'T USE HARSH PUNISHMENTS.
Washing a child's mouth out with soap for saying bad words simply causes a child to use the words out of his parents' earshot and doesn't teach a child appropriate humor substitutes. In other words, harsh punishment only drives his bad words underground so that you won't hear them . . . but someone will.

Ha-Ha vs. Hurt-Hurt

Nine-year-old Nick Vosler's sense of humor was one of his strong points, until he began trying to "gross out" his six-year-old brother. This entailed vividly describing the family's dinner menu in terms that his parents considered disgusting.

"Nick, it's not nice to say things like that!" Mr. and Mrs. Vosler would say, attempting to keep their son's humor within appropriate bounds.

Their admonishment didn't stop this budding comedian, however; so Mr. and Mrs. Vosler decided to institute a program to bring some control to their son's humor. First, they both agreed that Nick had the ability to cope with situations because he could find the humor in them. They wanted to protect his positive method of coping while doing something about the inappropriate direction that his humor seemed to be taking.

"Nick, we enjoy your sense of humor," Mr. Vosler told him before bed one evening. "You find the humor in almost any situation! But we do think some of the things you say to be funny are not appropriate. We've made a list of the things we consider off limits.

Nick and his father looked at the list together to make sure Nick understood the meanings of the words that were on it so he would understand why the words were off limits. The Voslers also told him, "Because you sometimes use insults to be funny, we have also decided to put a penalty on that kind of humor."

Nick began protesting. "But it's okay when they do that on television. Why can't I do it?"

"You're right. They do that on some of the programs you watch. Because this humor is not appropriate, we are going to restrict the shows you watch," his dad continued.

"That's not fair! I like those shows. Why can't I watch what I like?" Nick cried, becoming vocal in his fight for his rights.

"We understand that you like those shows, but they aren't good for you to watch right now. We won't let you watch some of the adult shows for that same reason. Nick, we want you to be safe and learn to do what's right. We aren't doing this just to be mean," his mother continued.

Mr. and Mrs. Vosler outlined the other facets of their plan, though Nick was not happy about them. When he used language from the off-limits list, he would be required to say the offending words for five minutes, his parents explained to him. When he insulted someone, he would be required to apologize to that person and to do a job to make up for hurting another person. Because they were focusing on offensive humor, they decided to ignore other forms of humor that were tasteless but not hurtful, and to laugh and comment on humor that was appropriate.

After wearing out a few of his favorite bodily function words and doing a few jobs, Nick began to learn what humor was appropriate and what wasn't. His parents still enjoyed his humor very much, and laughed with delight at his jokes and at the funny things he said and did. But they also were careful to follow through with the consequences if Nick broke the rules. This helped their son become more self-assured as he became more confident about how, when, and where to display the funny facet of his personality.

Teasing and Putting Others Down

("If I put *him* down, that will make *me* a better person!")

∧∧∧∧∧∧∧∧∧∧∧∧∧∧∧∧∧∧∧∧∧∧∧∧∧∧∧∧∧∧∧∧∧∧∧∧∧∧

The facts that a child who bullies others is not a troublemaker and that a victim does not need to fight back are hard to learn but important to teach childolescents who are victims of abuse from their peers. When your child cries "Johnny's teasing me" and "Mary's putting me down," help her to realize that her tormentor puts her down because he needs to feel powerful; because he cannot feel "up" about himself, he tries to one-up her. Use this same calm approach with your child if she bullies others. Teach her empathy by showing her how a person might feel when his feelings are hurt. At the same time, reward her for caring about the feelings of others. Both will pay off by helping her develop self-confidence to use when she makes her own choices and decisions, one of those being the decision not to hurt others.

PREVENTING THE PROBLEM

ENCOURAGE YOUR CHILD TO GET ALONG WITH OTHERS. A child will be less likely to tease or put her peers down if you make getting along with others a priority. The most direct way to encourage your child to get along with others is through praising her when she does.

MONITOR YOUR CHILD'S TELEVISION-VIEWING. The put-downs you hear on television may be funny, but when you hear them coming from your child's mouth, the humor fades. Allowing your child to watch programs in which the primary form of humor is putting people down only encourages her to use this form of humor herself.

TEACH APPROPRIATE USES OF POWER. The desire for power is the primary reason for teasing or putting down another person. Teach your child appropriate ways to exercise power by giving her experience in decision-making. Whenever possible, offer her choices. Say, "You may play nicely and get along with your friend or you may tease your friend and work for me. You choose how you want it to be."

MODEL COMPLIMENTARY BEHAVIOR. When you make a habit of saying complimentary things about people and their accomplishments, your child will be likely to do so as well.

SOLVING THE PROBLEM

What to Do

TEACH YOUR CHILD TO COPE WITH THE TEASING AND PUT-DOWNS OF OTHERS. When your child claims she is being made the scapegoat by one of her friends, ask, "What's the problem? The problem really is that you don't like being teased, isn't it?" If your child agrees with your problem diagnosis, ask, "When you don't like what others are doing, what are your choices of ways to react?" Then help your child generate a series of potential solutions to the problem:

PARENT: What are the choices?

CHILD: I could fight them!

PARENT: And if you did that, what would you expect would happen?

CHILD: They might hurt me.

PARENT: Would you want that?

CHILD: No.

PARENT: Okay, then, what else could you do?

CHILD: I could tell the teacher!

PARENT: What would you expect to happen if you did that?

CHILD: They would call me a tattletale.

PARENT: Do you want to do that?

CHILD: No.

PARENT: What else could you do?

CHILD: I could ignore them!

PARENT: Is that the one you think will work best?

CHILD: Yes!

If your child cannot come up with any solutions, help her by suggesting that she "ignore the other child's behavior." Then role-play using the solution with her to show her how the solution works. Say, "You be you and I'll be the teaser. Okay? Now here we go!" At that point, call your child names and have her say, "I don't like it when you do that." Then instruct her to walk away from you. Practice this role-playing until your child is comfortable with her chosen solution or solutions.

Note: It is important for a child to understand that she cannot have power over another person, only over herself, and that, if she is a victim of a bully, she has not done anything to cause anyone else to tease her.

MAKE RULES ABOUT THE TREATMENT OF OTHERS.

When your child begins teasing and putting others down, make a rule about how others should be treated. Tell your child, "The rule is: We treat others with kindness and respect." The most appropriate consequences to impose for violations of the no-teasing rule are restitutional jobs. Have her select a job card from your file (see JOB CARDS in "Discipline Dictionary.") This not only allows your child to make restitution for the crime committed, but also allows her to feel good about herself for doing something constructive.

PRAISE YOUR CHILD WHEN SHE TREATS OTHERS KINDLY. If your child is violating the rule about treating others kindly, praise those who *are* following the rule. This will encourage her to jump over to the praiseworthy side of the behavior fence.

What Not to Do

DON'T TEASE OR USE PUT-DOWNS YOURSELF. Don't get into the habit of teasing your child or using subtle put-downs in the form of pet names, such as "mean-machine." This will only encourage the same behavior from your child.

DON'T BECOME ANGRY WHEN YOUR CHILD TEASES. Allow your child to keep her self-respect while she learns to be more empathetic toward others.

DON'T BE OVERLY SYMPATHETIC. If your child complains about being teased or put down by other children, don't say, "Poor baby! I'm so sorry for you. Let me get you a brownie." Instead of giving her sympathy, help her develop her problem-solving skills and tease-tolerance.

DON'T TEASE YOUR CHILD JUST TO PROVE THAT TEASING HURTS. When you do, you will just be teaching your child how to tease.

∿∿∿∿∿∿∿∿∿∿∿∿∿∿∿∿∿∿∿∿∿∿∿

The Bully Meets His Match

Twelve-year-old Tommy Handleman was always teasing his classmates just to see them squirm. He created such inventive names that everyone thought he was hilarious—except his victims. Teasing gave Tommy power, an immediate reaction from his victims, and a loyal following who stuck by him in order to avoid being the targets of his cutting wit.

At home, however, Tommy was the victim. He had a teen-age brother who had been giving Tommy a hard time for years. Tommy felt as helpless at home as he felt powerful at school.

After several children became upset over Tommy's verbal abuse, Tommy's teacher sought help from the school counselor. Together with Tommy and his parents, the counselor devised a plan to help Tommy learn tease-tolerance as well as empathy for others.

First, she showed Tommy's parents how to reduce the teasing at home. They were instructed to comment on how nicely Tommy and his brothers were getting along when they played together amiably without teasing. If anyone teased anyone else, he had to work for the victim by doing the victim's chores for the day.

In addition, when Tommy *was* teased at home, his parents were to help him tolerate it by saying to himself, "It's no big deal. I can handle this. I'm not going to give my brother power over me." And if he resisted the teasing, he was praised and allowed special privileges.

To control Tommy's teasing others at school, a home-school communication system was devised by his parents, school counselor, and teacher. Tommy was instructed to carry a card at school which said, "I was kind to my classmates." At the end of the day, Tommy would meet with his teacher, and they would review his day. If it had gone by without teasing, he would put a check in the box for that day, and his teacher would initial the check. If he had teased someone, the box would be left blank.

When Tommy came home from school, he and his mother would review the card. If he had experienced a tease-free day, his mother would compliment him on his consideration for his classmates; then Tommy would get to play with his friends or do whatever else he wanted to do. If he had teased someone, he was given a chore to do.

In a short time, Tommy was teased much less at home. Moreover, he found he could cope with his brother's barbs whenever they were thrown at him. He also began treating his classmates much better at school, discovering that he didn't need to put others down in order to feel powerful. He already had power—over his own behavior and over how he chose to react to being teased.

School
Problems

〜〜〜〜〜〜〜〜〜〜〜〜〜〜〜〜〜〜〜〜〜〜〜〜〜〜〜〜〜〜〜〜〜〜

Breaking School Rules

("I don't care about the rule. I wanted to talk to Mark!")

∧∧∧∧∧∧∧∧∧∧∧∧∧∧∧∧∧∧∧∧∧∧∧∧∧∧∧∧∧∧∧∧∧∧

How helpless a parent feels on hearing the words, "Mrs. Jones, this is your son's teacher. I'm calling about his behavior." Perhaps your son broke a rule because he was angry about something his teacher did, because he believed a rule was unfair, or because breaking the rule brought him a lot of attention.

For whatever reason, if your child breaks a rule at school, consequences need to be enforced at home. It is only when your child understands that he must show self-control in school to receive the freedom he wants at home (and you work with teachers to establish this system) that he will be motivated to prevent bad-news phone calls from his teacher or principal.

PREVENTING THE PROBLEM

MAKE RULES IMPORTANT TO THE FAMILY.
Children who must stay within the boundaries of rules at home find it easier to conform to rules when they are away from home.

STATE RULES POSITIVELY. Rules should be stated as what to do rather than what not to do. The rule, "Get along with each other," tells children the behavior that you

want them to use and keeps that goal in their minds. On the other hand, the rule, "Don't fight," tells children what you *don't* want them to do and puts the undesirable behavior in the forefront of their minds.

MAKE A RULE CHART. Your child will remember rules better when he is reminded of them by seeing them posted. A family rule chart includes the major rules that you have established for your family and should state them positively.

PRAISE FOLLOWING RULES AT HOME AND AT SCHOOL. Offer your child encouragement each time that he follows a rule, to increase the likelihood of his wanting to follow the rule in the future. Say, "Thank you for remembering the rule," when he does so.

MODEL RULE-FOLLOWING. Talking about how ridiculous you think some rules are encourages your child to violate rules that he doesn't like. It is also difficult for him to see the value of rules when you consistently violate them. Point out times when you are following a rule (like stopping at a red traffic light) to remind your child that adults, as well as children, have to follow rules.

SOLVING THE PROBLEM

What to Do

SET UP A HOME-SCHOOL COMMUNICATION SYSTEM. If your child consistently violates school rules, establish a home-school communication system. The home-school system tells your child that his behavior at school will be known at home and that consequences will be given at home for behavior in school. In addition, it keeps you informed about your child's behavior during the day so you can thoroughly evaluate what may be causing his behavior to be so inappropriate. (See HOME-SCHOOL COMMUNICATION SYSTEM in the "Discipline Dictionary.")

SET UP CONSEQUENCES FOR FOLLOW-ING OR VIOLATING RULES. Based on the daily

message that you receive about your child's behavior from his teacher, at-home privileges can be granted or taken away. When your child follows a school rule and requests the freedom to go to a friend's house to play after school, say, "Because you have shown that you can follow a rule at school, I believe that I can trust you to follow a home rule about going to Jim's house. You may go to Jim's; please call me when you want to come home, and I will pick you up." This offer of parental trust and freedom fosters self-confidence in a child and helps to strengthen parent-child relationships.

When a school rule is not followed, tell your child, "I'm sorry that you didn't follow the rule." Then ask him, "What can you do tomorrow so that you can remember to follow the rule?" Finally, remind him of the consequences he will now receive because he did not follow the rule.

The most appropriate negative consequence for children who violate school rules is to assign them jobs to do. Children who work to make restitution for violating school rules learn to do something constructive to make up for the violation and, in turn, learn to feel good about themselves after completing a job satisfactorily. Say, "Because you chose to talk out loud in class every day this week, you must pick five job cards to do, one for every day after school, starting today."

What Not to Do

DON'T PUT SCHOOL DOWN. Often parents be-

lieve that the school rules being violated are silly and need not be obeyed. Just because you don't agree with a rule, however, doesn't mean that your child should not follow it. Rather than encouraging fights with the school over the appropriateness of a rule, teach your child that rules are important to follow and that there are reasons for having them.

Note: You can, of course, discuss school rules with teachers and school administrators to see if they are interested in changing or amending a rule with which you disagree.

DON'T OVERREACT TO THE PROBLEM. Becoming angry and using harsh punishment at home (such as spanking, yelling, and grounding) for school-rule violations doesn't teach your child how to obey rules. Instead, it teaches him to avoid you because he sees you as harsh and punitive. Harsh punishment also fosters resentment. Instead of getting out of control, set reasonable consequences for your child's following rules as well as for his violating them.

~~~~~~~~~~~~~~~~~~~~~~~~~~~~~~~~~~

The High Cost of Freedom

Guilt had seized Zach Halleran's mother since she had begun getting calls from her son's third-grade teacher about his behavior in school. She had felt so sorry for Zach's having to grow up without a dad (she and Zach's father were divorced), and was so tired when she got home each night, that she had begun to let him get away with behavior that she knew she should be correcting.

But after receiving a fourth bad-behavior report from school in one week, she knew that she had to take action. And when his teacher called about the fifth transgression, she made an appointment for a conference with her. His mother and teacher asked Zach to attend the conference so that he would understand that they were united in their efforts to improve his behavior.

"Zach, we are having this meeting so we can help you stay out of trouble in school," his teacher began. "I'm sure you don't like to get into trouble all the time, either."

"I like it!" Zach announced defiantly.

"Now, Zach, don't talk like that! We're here to help you," his mother reprimanded.

"Zach, here is the plan," his teacher quickly broke in, as she handed him a piece of paper. "We are going to send this form home each day with you."

Zach read a few of the rules that they wanted him to follow, such as: I stayed in my seat; I raised my hand to talk; I did my best work; and I respected my classmates.

"Zach, you will rate how well you followed the rules in class every day, then bring the paper to me, and I will rate your rule-following behavior, too. At the end of the day, you can take the paper home to your mother, and she will pay you for every one of the rules that you have followed that day."

"What do you mean, she'll pay me?" Zach asked.

"She will give you tokens; with the tokens you can buy things to do. Here is a list of the things that you can buy and the cost of each," his teacher explained. Zach saw that the list included playtime, television-viewing, video game-playing time, and other things he liked to do.

"Do you mean that I'll have to *buy* all of these things now?" he inquired.

"Yes, Zach," his mother replied. "But it shouldn't be hard. You'll earn a lot of tokens by following the rules here at school."

"It's not fair!" Zach cried.

"Zach, will you agree to try the program for a week?" his teacher wanted to know.

Reluctantly, Zach agreed. Because he decided to go along with the program, he was given ten bonus tokens. Not bad, he thought.

By the end of the week, he was really enjoying the system. He had earned enough tokens to have his best friend spend the night on Saturday, something his mother had usually refused to allow because she didn't like the noise that the boys made. In addition, Zach was able to earn bonus tokens by going to bed at a reasonable time and by being less rambunctious while his friend was over.

By the end of the semester, this token system had died of disuse. Zach's behavior was consistently good at school, and he had learned the consequences of exercising self-control. He was enjoying being a good student and being liked by his teacher; his breaking school rules was just a bad memory.

Poor Study Habits

("I can't finish this homework. I'm not even going to try!")

∿∿∿∿∿∿∿∿∿∿∿∿∿∿∿∿∿∿∿∿∿∿∿∿∿∿∿∿∿∿∿

The belief that schoolwork is something to avoid seems to invade a child's psyche by the second or third grade. Not coincidentally, this is when a child begins to receive grades—comparative ratings on her work. As with any competitive activity, how a child performs in school affects her feelings about how successful and capable she is.

Teach your child that taking the risk of trying makes her a winner, because she cannot make the grade, literally, unless she tries. Reward even small steps your child takes in the process of doing schoolwork—remembering to bring her book home or paying attention while the teacher is giving a lesson, for example—to motivate her to pick up habits that will help her feel good about her school efforts. Each child's intelligence, creativity, and ability to reason is unique. Discover what subjects or skills present the greatest challenges to your child and then, together with your child's teacher, establish a step-by-step plan to help her meet those challenges. With your child making the effort and you playing the role of helper, she will come to view school as a can-do proposition.

PREVENTING THE PROBLEM

TALK WITH YOUR CHILD'S TEACHERS. It is of vital importance for you to meet your child's classroom teacher. Ask the teacher questions, such as, What is my child's learning style? What time of day is she most tuned out? With what subjects or skills does she have to struggle? What resources are available within the school for more extensive diagnosis and treatment? Based on what you learn from her teacher, develop a plan for ways to help your child correct each situation.

MAKE LEARNING A FAMILY PRIORITY. A
child who sees that her parents enjoy learning is more likely to enjoy learning herself. You can establish a learning atmosphere by discussing current events, reading, providing stimulating books and magazines, taking your child to museums, and praising her learning efforts.

ENCOURAGE QUESTIONING. When your child
is allowed to ask questions, such as, "Why does Grandpa smoke?", "When are we going on vacation?", or "Where does hamburger come from?" she is being encouraged to seek knowledge, an important motivation in being a diligent student.

LIMIT TELEVISION-VIEWING TIME. A child
who becomes addicted to the passive activity of watching television will eventually expect knowledge to be given to her rather than learning to seek it out. Learning is an active process, which requires the expenditure of energy, so give your child practice outside of school in activities such as reading, writing stories, and playing learning games, instead of watching television.

ENCOURAGE CREATIVITY. When your child cre-
ates anything, from a picture to a model plane or a poem, praise the effort that she put into the work rather than the outcome. Say, "I really like how you concentrated on drawing that picture." Creativity is also nurtured by holding brainstorming sessions to devise a variety of solutions to a problem.

HELP YOUR CHILD TAKE PRIDE IN MAKING THE EFFORT TO DO SOMETHING. When
good grades come home, encourage your child to take pride
in the effort she made to get those grades. Say, "You must be
so proud of that grade! That took a lot of work to achieve."
This helps her understand that the grade belongs to her, and
she didn't do the work for *you* to be proud. It was *her* work
done for *her*.

MODEL ORGANIZATION. Make sure you are or-
ganized; sometimes a child finds it difficult to get and stay
organized when she doesn't see examples of organization
around her all the time.

ENCOURAGE LISTENING. You can encourage the
development of the listening skills that are necessary for following directions in school by asking your child questions
about conversations, television programs, and teacher instructions. Other fun ways to build listening skills are by
playing games, such as Simple Simon, and listening to and
repeating the rhythm and words to songs. In addition, invite
your child to contribute her own ideas to conversations so you
can model listening skills for her, too.

REWARD TASK-COMPLETION. Your child may
not always see the benefit of finishing the things she starts.
But by setting up rewards for the completion of chores, homework, and other activities, you teach her that sticking with
something to the end pays off. When you insist that your child
not quit an activity that involves hard work, you encourage
her to see things through to their conclusion.

SOLVING THE PROBLEM

What to Do

HELP YOUR CHILD SET REASONABLE GOALS.

Set step-by-step goals that your child can accomplish. Making top grades (or even a top grade in one subject) may not be a goal your child can attain, but the goal of completing ten arithmetic problems may be possible. After deciding what is a reasonable academic subject goal, offer your child a reward for reaching it. Say, "When you have completed ten math problems, then you may call your friend and talk for five minutes." You may increase the number of problems required for five minutes of free time by adding up to two problems a day.

SET A REASONABLE STUDY TIME.

The best study time for an underachiever is immediately after school. This allows the remainder of the evening to be used as leverage to encourage her to do the required work and then be rewarded by having her evening free.

BREAK STUDY TIME INTO SMALL BLOCKS.

Have your child do the most difficult or least-liked task first, then follow its completion with a short "fun" break. This makes study time pass more quickly and pleasantly for your child. After finishing that worst task, your child should do the next most difficult or hated task, followed by another break, and so on until her homework is completed.

SET ASIDE A GOOD STUDY AREA.

Your child may want to do homework in her room, but her room may also be filled with distractions that seem to leap up on the pages to be studied. A study area devoid of stimulation where she can easily concentrate on her work is best.

ESTABLISH A HOME-SCHOOL COMMUNICATION SYSTEM.

Unless you know what your child's homework assignment is, it is difficult for you to ensure that her work gets done. A simple assignment notebook that is completed by your child, verified by her teacher's signature, and brought home every day is the best tool to safeguard against "homework breakdown."

Using an assignment notebook also encourages your child to be responsible for keeping track of her own assignments. Create this rule about using the notebook: When your child's assignment notebook comes home, she needs to do her homework. After the homework is done, she can then have free time. If she does not bring home the assignment notebook, she must do make-up problems in her weakest subject. In other words, you create the homework if she forgets to bring home her assignment notebook. If your child brings home her assignments, but not the notebook, then she is required to do those assignments as well as the homework you invent.

SET UP A DAILY HOME-SCHOOL NOTE SYSTEM WITH YOUR CHILD'S TEACHER.

It is next to impossible for you to help your child improve her study habits if you don't know her daily school routines. Set up a daily home-school note to help your child's teacher encourage her to do good work. The note should include a list of your child's goals in school, such as listening, completing work, and keeping the work organized.

Your child should rate her own behavior daily and then ask her teacher to verify her rating. Her teacher then marks the note appropriately and gives it back to your child to take home at the end of the day. Reward all good marks on the note by granting your child privileges and praising her efforts.

USE CHECKLISTS FOR ORGANIZATION.

Some children just seem to be born disorganized. To establish good organization habits at home, your student needs a checklist to remind her of the tasks needed to be done in an organized sequence.

Note: Some children have learning disabilities that make it difficult for them to listen, follow directions, complete tasks, and behave in an organized fashion. If your child seems always to have problems focusing on learning, contact her school or physician for referral to a specialist.

What Not to Do

DON'T ARGUE ABOUT HOMEWORK. If your child refuses to do her homework, say, "I'm sorry you have refused to do your English assignment. That means you also have refused to let yourself play, watch television, eat, or do any of the other things you like to do." Then be calm and patient as your child reevaluates whether or not to do her homework; finally, enforce the consequences of her decision.

DON'T CORRECT YOUR CHILD'S HOME-WORK. A child must learn to do her work and accept the grades that she has earned. Your correcting homework rescues your child from that responsibility.

DON'T THREATEN. Saying, "If you don't bring your grades up, you will be grounded!" only tells your child that she may soon be in trouble. It doesn't give her a way to improve her grades. Instead, say, "I'm sorry your grades aren't as good as you are capable of getting. Here is the plan we will follow." Outlining the plan cited earlier in this chapter will help bring her grades up to her level of capability.

DON'T INSIST ON ACADEMIC PERFEC-TION. No one is capable of perfection. If errors are made on an assignment, pointing out the correct answers and asking your child to correct her errors allows her to learn. Encouraging your child's effort is better than demanding perfection.

DON'T PAY FOR GRADES WITH MONEY.

The efforts that a child makes in school on a daily basis should be rewarded on a daily basis through your granting her privileges, such as being able to play or watch a reasonable amount of television after her homework is done. Paying for grades at report-card time doesn't reflect the nine weeks of effort that went into the achievement because the relationship between the effort and the reward is lost. Equating money or tangible rewards with grades also creates the expectation that learning should be rewarded rather than the idea that learning is rewarding.

DON'T PUNISH YOUR CHILD FOR LOW GRADES.

Children who are punished only learn how to avoid the punisher, not how to correct the problem. Grounding your child because she doesn't listen in school only encourages her to lie and to hide the fact that she may not listen; it won't teach her good study habits.

DON'T NAG ABOUT HOMEWORK.

A child views her parents' asking if she has homework as their nagging her to do it. A child will often lie and say she doesn't have any work to do, just to stop the nagging. Instead of nagging, stick to the routine of where, when, and how homework is to be done every day.

DON'T FOCUS ON GRADES.

A child needs to learn to give her best effort, not to work for grades. However, don't remind your child to "do her best," because she will interpret that remark as meaning "be perfect!"—an unattainable goal.

DON'T CRITICIZE INCORRECT SCHOOLWORK.

Instead of criticizing your child's incorrect schoolwork, praise the parts of her work that have been done correctly and ask her to upgrade the remainder of the work to that standard. Say, "You really did well on this part. Now see if you can make the other part of your math assignment look as good."

~~~~~~

Reading, Writing, and Runke

Peter Runke was something of a procrastinator, always putting off things that his parents thought were important, including doing his homework.

Peter's parents first became concerned about his procrastinating habit, however, when his teacher called and asked them to come in for a conference. During the meeting, the teacher said that Peter was bright, but he was not good at following through with his work. "Peter is old enough to be responsible," she continued, "but he isn't choosing to take that responsibility. So we need to help him learn how to do what he needs to do."

They planned how they would teach Peter to take responsibility for his schoolwork. That evening, Peter's parents sat down with him and outlined the new plan.

"Peter, we had a meeting with your teacher today. We all want to help you be a successful student. Here is what we are going to do," his father began.

First, they set a study time each day immediately after school so that Peter would want to finish his work and get time to play. But Peter balked at having study time right after school. "I want to play with my friends after school. By the time I get done with my homework, it'll be dinnertime and everybody will be in by then," he protested.

"I understand, Peter," his father answered. "Now, how much time do you think your homework will take?"

"About a half hour, I guess, if I don't mess around," Peter answered.

"Then if you get home at three forty-five, you could be finished by four fifteen or four thirty at the latest. Now, dinner isn't until six o'clock, so it looks like you could have at least an hour and a half of playtime before you have to come in. Is that fair enough?" his father asked.

Peter assented, and their conference continued. A daily communication system would be set up, with Peter recording his assignments each day and his teacher signing his assignment notebook to verify what he had to do. His parents would match his completed homework with his assignment notebook every day.

After the quarterly grades came out showing that Peter had improved in all subjects, his teacher shifted from a daily to a weekly progress report. Because Peter knew that his having free time was based on his doing his schoolwork, he eagerly kept his part of the contract, as his parents kept theirs.

Getting Up and Out on Time

("I don't want to get up and face such a hard day!")

∿∿∿∿∿∿∿∿∿∿∿∿∿∿∿∿∿∿∿∿∿∿∿∿∿∿∿

Many middle-years children stay under the covers after the alarm goes off to avoid facing unpleasant responsibilities, people, or places . . . or simply to catch up on their sleep after a slumber party or restless night full of nightmares. Find out why your child is becoming a sleepyhead: Ask him about his day to see if there is anything bothering him, and review bedtime policies to see if his current routines are out of sync with his sleep needs. Then encourage your child to rise and shine by praising his slightest movements toward that morning goal.

Some children are simply not at their peak in the morning. So, streamline chores for a child who thrives on a slower morning routine. For example, play wardrobe and prop director at night by planning what clothes he will wear and what school books he will take the next day.

PREVENTING THE PROBLEM

KEEP THE SCHEDULE TIGHT. When your child has too much time in the morning in which to get ready for school, he doesn't feel the need to move along. He often ends up being late in spite of the ample time he had in which to get dressed and eat breakfast. Limit the amount of time he has in which to get ready to keep moving toward the "getting ready" goal.

ENCOURAGE YOUR CHILD TO GO TO BED ON TIME. Decide on a reasonable bedtime and stick to it to prevent early morning sleepiness. A getting-ready-for-bed routine helps, as well.

DO HOMEWORK AND OTHER PROJECTS EARLY. Staying up late to complete homework is counter-productive, because a child cannot make his best effort when he is exhausted. Make sure your child gets his homework done early in the evening so he can relax and prepare for sleep when the time comes.

MAKE SURE YOUR CHILD EXERCISES. Getting good exercise during the day helps your child's body get good rest at night so he can feel rested in the morning.

DISCUSS THE DAY'S PROBLEMS AT THE DAY'S END. Children who try to sleep when they're worried will not feel rested in the morning. Problem-solving before going to sleep can help your child feel comfortable and secure about facing the new day. Before bedtime say, "Let's talk about your day. Tell me some good things that happened."

PUT YOUR CHILD IN CHARGE. Encourage your child to take the responsibility for getting himself up in the morning. Give him the tool to do so—an alarm clock or clock radio—and let him set his own wake-up call.

CLEARLY DEFINE YOUR CHILD'S NEEDS TO BE UP AND AROUND. Because some children move more quickly than others, each child's schedule should be individualized. A morning checklist helps a child know

when he needs to be done with one activity and proceed to another. This also helps put the responsibility of getting up and ready on your child and off of you.

GET THINGS READY THE NIGHT BEFORE.

Encourage your child to select the clothes that he will be wearing the following day, as well as the school books and papers that he will be needing. This allows extra time to find library books that may be "hidden" or sew on buttons that may be missing. In this way, your child will be more prepared as he gets ready for his day.

ASSIGN ONLY MORNING CHORES THAT ARE RELATED TO GOING TO SCHOOL, CAMP, OR OTHER MORNING ACTIVITIES.

SOLVING THE PROBLEM

What to Do

USE A GENTLE WAKE-UP ROUTINE. A child

who wakes gently with loving encouragement from you will be more inclined to want to get up and face his day. Talking to your child in a soft voice and using a gentle touch to rouse him avoids the unpleasant feelings stimulated by a harsh wake-up buzzer alarm on a radio. Some children find it so much more pleasant to be awakened gently that their better frame of mind makes them more cooperative, in general.

PLAY BEAT THE CLOCK. Once your child is awake,

set the kitchen timer for a certain number of minutes. Then give him this contract: "Let's see if you can beat the clock getting up and coming to breakfast," or "For getting yourself

up and ready on time, you'll be able to play after school."
The excitement of competition will serve to motivate your
child to move toward the getting-up goal.

ASK YOUR CHILD ABOUT HIS SCHEDULE FOR THE DAY.

Sometimes a child avoids getting up in
the morning because he wants to avoid confronting a person
or experience awaiting him. Ask, "What is your day going to
be like? Is there anything going to happen today that you
won't enjoy?" If you discover that your child is dreading facing the problems ahead of him, then work on problem-
solving. (See PROBLEM-SOLVING in the "Discipline Dictionary.")

STAY WITH THE SLOW-MOVER.

A child whose
motor takes some time to get going in the morning may need
more encouragement from parents while he stretches and gets
himself up. Sit on the bed with your child while praising any
of his movements toward the goal of getting up and dressed.
Say, "I can see you're getting up now and going to be ready
on time," to encourage your child toward the goal.

What Not to Do

DON'T MAKE EARLY MORNING A BATTLE-GROUND.

Children will be more willing to get up and
get started if the morning begins on a pleasant note.

DON'T MAKE A HABIT OF BEING LATE YOURSELF IN THE MORNING.

Model being on
time to show your child that it's an important goal.

DON'T THREATEN.

Your child will learn very quickly
that your bark is worse than your bite if you threaten him by
saying, "If you don't get up, your teachers are going to be
mad at you." Threats may motivate a child to take immediate
action, but they don't teach him how to get up on time.

AVOID PHYSICAL BATTLES. Physically dragging a child out of bed increases the chances of major conflicts in the morning, including the use of physical violence on your child's part.

DON'T BE A HISTORIAN. Reminding your child that he should have gone to bed earlier the night before will neither motivate him to get up in the morning nor motivate him to go to bed earlier the next night.

Monica's Morning Misery

Monica Carlson's father would beg, plead, threaten, and cajole his daughter to leave her bunk bed behind each morning; but the louder he warned her that she would be late for school, the longer this nine-year-old would stay in bed.

One morning, after a particularly nasty battle, Monica's father said, "That's it. I've had enough. I'm not going to fight with you every morning. When I come home tonight, we are going to make a new rule about getting up in the morning."

Monica had been through this before, but all the threats had amounted to nothing. So she wasn't worried.

After school, she had her snack, and then she sat down with her father as he outlined the new plan. "I'm going to let you get yourself up in the morning by using this clock radio I no longer use. You set it for the time that you think you should get up so that you can make it to the school bus on time. From now on, getting up will be your responsibility. When you have accepted this responsibility, you will then be free to play with your friends, watch television, or do anything you want within the house rules. If you choose not to be responsible, I will get you up when I'm ready to go to work and take you to school so you won't be late, regardless of whether you're ready."

Monica looked at her father in disbelief. "You mean, you'll

drag me out of bed and take me to school the way I am?" Monica could only try to picture her father shoving her out of the car at school while she was still wearing her pajamas. "You wouldn't!" she said.

"We would just take your clothes with you so you could get dressed in the car or at school," he answered quietly. "You get to choose how you want to handle this situation."

From then on, Monica got up to her radio alarm and was dressed and ready to eat breakfast by the time she had to catch the school bus. She almost refused to get up once, but it suddenly hit her that time was going by and her father wasn't coming to get her up. She jumped out of bed and pulled on her clothes. She was too late to eat breakfast, but was on time for the bus.

Monica and her father both agreed that their mornings were much sunnier without a fight. And Monica really felt grown up with her own alarm and her newfound responsibility.

Noise

Swearing and Using Bad Language

("I know a word that will really make everyone listen to me!")

$\wedge$

The shock value of swearing and bad language is one of the monumental discoveries a child makes between the ages of six and twelve. It is monumental because it wreaks havoc on parents' sensibilities to hear their heretofore sweet, innocent child uttering vulgarities. To clean up your child's new act, try to downplay your reaction to the verbal garbage that he is bringing home. First see if he actually knows what the sinful sounds mean. Allow him to state his own definition of a swear word, then tell him whether the word has been correctly or incorrectly used and defined. In short, take the allure out of using swear words and teach your child that he can safely discuss his bad language lessons, as well as his good ones, with you.

PREVENTING THE PROBLEM

MONITOR FRIENDS. A child will often select friends who use language that his parents don't like. Because you can't really enforce all restrictions on these friends, enforce this rule: Your child can play with certain friends (those not on your "favorite" list) only at your house where you can hear their language and monitor it.

ESTABLISH RULES ABOUT THE USE OF BAD LANGUAGE. It is important for you to share with your

child your philosophy about using certain words. When your child uses bad language, ask him how he feels about it. Say, "How does saying that word make you feel? What should you say instead of the 'off-limits' word?" Finally, remind him of the house rule about swearing. Make sure that you tell your child that you love him, but not his using those words.

TALK ABOUT WHAT WORDS MEAN. Your child needs to know what language is acceptable and what is offensive in our society in order to avoid getting in trouble. So when your child questions the meaning and use of a particular word, explain why it is unacceptable and what the consequences will be for using it.

SET AN EXAMPLE FOR YOUR CHILD. A child who hears parents using appropriate language will most likely use the same language because it is familiar to him.

DEFINE LANGUAGE PARAMETERS BY MAKING A LIST OF APPROPRIATE AND INAPPROPRIATE WORDS. Help your child learn acceptable words and praise him when he uses them appropriately.

SOLVING THE PROBLEM

What to Do

WEAR OUT BAD WORDS. When you overhear your child using an offensive word, have him repeat the word for five minutes. He will tire of the word very quickly and be more likely to give up using it. If he refuses to repeat the word for five minutes as you tell him to do, simply inform him that he can do what he likes after he has paid this penalty for using bad words.

PRAISE THE USE OF APPROPRIATE LANGUAGE.
When your child has the opportunity to use bad language but chooses good language instead, his self-control should be praised. This reinforcement will encourage your child to repeat his performance to get more applause in the future.

What Not to Do

DON'T BECOME SHOCKED AND ANGRY WHEN BAD WORDS ARE USED.
Your child loves power, and using bad language makes him powerful if you overreact to the words he is using. Keep your own angry language under control so your child won't end up controlling you.

DON'T USE SEVERE PUNISHMENT FOR BAD WORDS.
Washing a child's mouth out with soap may clean up his mouth, but it won't clean up his language. If you punish your child in this way (or by spanking, shouting, or threatening), he only learns how to avoid getting caught using bad language by taking it "underground," away from punishers like you.

∿∿∿∿∿∿∿∿∿∿∿∿∿∿∿∿∿∿∿∿∿∿∿∿

On the Offensive

Ten-year-old Jeremy Sumner had gained quite a reputation around his neighborhood and on the school playground as the "kid with the bad mouth"—a reputation that made him feel strong and grown-up.

Eventually, Jeremy's notoriety got back to his parents, who, beset by anger and embarrassment, sat him down and gave him a lecture. "Don't you know how embarrassing it is to hear about the language you are using around the neighborhood?" they cried. "Aren't you ashamed of your behavior? Well, what do you have to say for yourself?"

Jeremy had nothing to say, so they tried the traditional punishment for swearing—washing his mouth out with soap. After forcing their son to sit for five minutes with a bar of soap in his mouth, they considered the matter resolved.

But word of Jeremy's verbal offenses continued to filter back. He was being more careful to avoid getting caught by adults, but his bad language was being reported by other children.

Jeremy's parents decided that they had to change tactics. They remembered that when Jeremy was younger, he had only wanted to eat hot dogs—for every meal. One day, he got into the refrigerator and ate a whole package. From then on, he wouldn't eat another hot dog.

His parents decided to use the same overkill technique on Jeremy's language problem. In order for him to know what language was considered inappropriate, Jeremy and his parents made a list of "forbidden" words. The next time Mr. and Mrs. Sumner heard reports that he had used a word from the list, Mrs. Sumner said, "It appears that you like that word, so I want you to sit here and repeat it as loudly and fast as you can until the timer rings."

"I won't do it!" he answered defiantly, and he sat in the designated chair, his arms folded across his chest, with his jaw set.

"I understand," Mrs. Sumner calmly replied. "Now let me tell you what the deal is. You can sit there forever if you want, or you can say the word for five minutes and be able to get up and do what you would like to do. You decide how you want it to be."

Jeremy sat for a while, but then his parents heard him start saying the offending word.

This scenario was repeated a few more times until Jeremy decided that using the forbidden words was hardly worth the price he had to pay; and his vocabulary improved to prove it!

Complaining

("I never get to do anything!")

~~~~~~

Children in the middle years tend to focus on the extremes of life, to be perfectionists, and to lack tolerance for things that don't fit their notion of how the world should be. Words that express judgments such as "hate," "awful," and "never" are central players in their vocabulary. Complaining is thus a way in which they express this developmentally normal (albeit hard to tolerate!) view of the world.

When your child's complaining begins to color everything in her world black, though, she is reflecting a depressed mood that may ultimately be damaging to her.

But these childolescents are still looking for payoffs, just as they did when they were preschoolers. So parents, beware! When your child complains, watch your reaction. Instead of responding directly to her complaining—which encourages her to see the world as negative and difficult—teach your child to focus on the enjoyable aspects of life and reward her behavior through giving attention to this new, positive view. This is not to say that you need *only* to encourage a positive attitude. What is important is to encourage problem-solving as an alternative to complaining, which only focuses on what *can't* be done rather than what *can*.

Note: Beware of a big source of childolescents' complaints—other people's behavior. An important part of problem-solving is teaching a child that she cannot control the behavior of others, but she can control what she thinks about that behavior.

PREVENTING THE PROBLEM

SET UP A POSITIVE ATMOSPHERE AT HOME. When a child lives in a home in which the world is viewed in a positive way, she tends to see the world in the same way. You can encourage this positive view by discussing issues in a noncomplaining way and approaching problems with the attitude that they can be solved.

BRAINSTORM SOLUTIONS WITH YOUR CHILD. Define what the problem is that your child is complaining about and, with your child, decide upon a list of potential solutions. Then evaluate each solution in terms of its outcome potential and help her choose the one that offers the most favorable possible outcome.

HELP YOUR CHILD APPRECIATE LIFE. When your child complains about the unfriendly behavior of her teacher, say, "Yes, I understand how you feel about your teacher acting irritable, but she may be under a lot of stress. Maybe if you try to understand that something must be bothering her and help her have a better day, she will be less cranky."

The following appreciative view also models for a child how she can think in positive ways about her life (rather than focusing on the negative and ending up feeling sorry for herself). For example, when your child complains about not being able to play with a friend, say, "You have such nice friends. You must be happy to be able to play with them as much as you do. Even if you can't be with your friend today, I'll bet you can find something interesting to do; and if you can't, I have some jobs for you to do."

SOLVING THE PROBLEM

What to Do

PLAY THE "GOOD DAY" GAME. The "good day" game encourages players to adopt a positive view of the world by requiring them to tell their parents five good things that happened on a particular day. If your child refuses to play, enforce Grandma's Rule (see "Discipline Dictionary"). Say, "When you have thought of five good things, then you may go play or do whatever you would like."

BE EMPATHETIC. When a child's complaints seem genuine, be understanding of the feelings involved. Say, "I understand how you feel. It must have been tough not to have had anyone to sit with on the bus. It looks like we need to work on solving that problem." By being empathetic, not sympathetic, you teach your child that complaining doesn't solve problems, but coming up with solutions does.

REWARD TOLERANCE. When your overly critical child is complaining about someone or something, reward her when she stops her unpleasant utterances by saying, "It sounds so much better when you aren't complaining." Praising the absence of complaining by saying, "You have been so tolerant of things recently. Thanks!", will also increase the likelihood of your child's critical behavior becoming extinct.

PUT PENALTIES ON INTOLERANCE. When your critical child puts something or somebody down, impose a penalty. Say, for example, "I'm sorry you were speaking unkindly about Matthew. You will have to do a job for me now to make up for that." This teaches a child that complaining about others is costly and that it pays to speak kindly!

LOOK FOR SELF-PITY. When people feel sorry for themselves, they will often end up feeling depressed. Their view of the world is negative and the fun is gone from life.

If your child is constantly complaining about things, look for what might be causing her self-pity, and then try to help your child drop the pity posture. Say, "Yes, I understand that you are lonely because your best friend moved. Now, what is more fun to think about than feeling sorry that your friend left?"

POINT OUT THE "GOOD" IN THINGS. Try to help your child see all sides (both positive and negative) to a personal situation, as well as to an issue. Your child's saying, "She's gross!" when describing her teacher can be countered by your saying to your child, "First tell me some good things about your teacher."

What Not to Do

DON'T BE OVERLY SYMPATHETIC. Saying, "Oh, you poor thing," when your child complains, only encourages her to complain in order to get parental sympathy. Instead, ask, "What do you think you might do about that?" This encourages your child to think of solutions to a problem and not dwell on the problem itself.

AVOID BECOMING UPSET BY YOUR CHILD'S COMPLAINING. Overreacting to your child's comments can be a subtle put-down of your child, because it suggests that your child is wrong about what she said. Your child wasn't wrong; her view of the world was just a negative one. Therefore, rather than becoming upset, impose penalties on criticizing and help your child see all sides (both good and bad) of people and situations, as you avoid being critical of her.

Closing the Complaint Department

Carrie Thompson had been a generally happy girl, so her mother became concerned when she started complaining about school, her friends, teachers, her mother's meals, and her little brother. Since she turned eight, it seemed that nothing was satisfying to her anymore.

One evening at dinner, Carrie looked at the meal that her mother had prepared, turned up her nose, and exclaimed, "Yuk! I hate this!"

Her mother finally exploded. "Do you know how long I worked to fix this meal? Just leave the table, young lady. You can come back when you learn to appreciate what others do for you."

Carrie stormed off in tears and spent the evening in her room.

Her parents held a caucus to formulate a plan. "Look, I think we're making too big a deal out of her complaints. Maybe if we just ignored them for a while, they would stop," Carrie's father suggested. They decided not only to ignore the complaints, but to teach Carrie how to cope better with the trials and tribulations of life.

The next day after school, Carrie stormed into the house. "My teacher is so dumb. She expects us to be quiet all the time and never talk or we get our name on the board. I hate her!" Carrie moaned.

"Carrie, I don't want to hear about that now. Instead, I want to hear five good things that happened today," her mother calmly countered.

"Good things? Nothing good happened today. I can't think of any good things," Carrie retorted in a huff.

"That's okay, sweetheart," her mother replied. "But I would like you to sit with me until you can think of five good things that happened. While we are waiting, I'll tell you a good thing that happened to me. Mrs. Johnson called today to tell me how much she enjoyed the card we sent her when she was sick. Wasn't that nice of her?"

"Well, Samantha told me this morning that she thought my shirt was really neat," Carrie ventured.

"That was nice of her," her mother responded.

After a few minutes, Carrie and her mother had come up with many good things to say about Carrie's day, and she hurried off to play in a much better mood.

Later in the week, a true problem came up, and Carrie and her mother confronted it together. They decided what the problem was, talked about some possible solutions, and chose a solution that seemed workable. Carrie seemed satisfied about the outcome of that particular problem, as well as about her life in general—returning to her happier behavior patterns and enabling her parents to return to theirs.

Arguing and Talking Back

("I'll show you who's boss!")

∿∿∿∿∿∿∿∿∿∿∿∿∿∿∿∿∿∿∿∿∿∿∿∿∿∿∿

More than any other verbal games that children play during the middle years, talking back and arguing seem to offend parents the most. The effect of these noises allows children to feel powerful. Arguing also gives them a way of testing their ability to think and reason. Assume the role of benevolent dictator when your child mouths off about cleaning his dishes off the dinner table by calmly giving him these two choices: He can clean off his dishes and then go play, or not do so and not be able to play as he wants. By giving your child experience in making these kinds of choices and accepting the consequences of his choice, you are giving him the power he craves in an appropriate way. You are also communicating the healthy message that if he respects authority figures in his life and helps meet their goals, they will help him meet his goals.

PREVENTING THE PROBLEM

BE CONSISTENT. Your child will respond best to parental authority when he knows how you will react. When you are consistent, your child feels little need to test the rules because he already knows the test results.

TREAT YOUR CHILD WITH RESPECT. If you give your child the respect he deserves, he is more likely to treat you with the same respect. Using appropriate language is one way of respecting others. Model speaking respectfully to your child. Swearing, name-calling, and yelling are all demeaning behaviors that show a lack of respect.

PREVENT ARGUING BY ALLOWING VIEWS TO BE AIRED. Allow your child to air his views and to agree to disagree. Views should be aired at a neutral time, such as at a family meeting, where thoughts can be expressed openly without criticism.

SOLVING THE PROBLEM

What to Do

SET HOUSE RULES. House rules should be set so that the rule becomes the authority to follow or disobey instead of you. A house rule could be, "We use nice language, treat each other with respect, and discuss and negotiate instead of argue." If, for example, one of your child's family jobs is to clear his dishes from the dinner table, and he asks rebelliously, "Why do I have to?", say, "I understand that you may not want to follow this rule now, but it is important to follow it so that we keep the house neat." Don't say "Clear the table because I said so!" This will only encourage your child to test your authority and start a verbal battle with you.

CONSIDER BACK TALK AND A SMART MOUTH AS NOISE. You may think that your child is being disrespectful when you hear him using back talk; but in reality, he is only testing his power over his world. If you consider back talk to be noise coming from your child's mouth and refuse to respond to it, the noise will soon go away. When your child says, "I hate you! I want another mother!", calmly say, "I'm sorry you've chosen to feel that way," and go about

your business, leaving your child to select more positive ways of getting your attention.

PUT A PENALTY ON ARGUING. You can discourage arguing by raising its cost. Make it a rule that arguing time is sold at the going rate of one job per minute of arguing time. With this rule to play by, most children quickly decide that arguing is not worth its cost.

TEACH YOUR CHILD TO NEGOTIATE FOR WHAT HE WANTS. Your child will choose to negotiate rather than argue for what he wants when he finds that it benefits him to do so. (See NEGOTIATION in the "Discipline Dictionary.")

What Not to Do

DON'T USE BELITTLING LANGUAGE. Don't speak to your child rudely. Avoid saying things like "Shut up!" and, "Don't be a jerk!"

DON'T BECOME ANGRY IF YOUR CHILD TESTS THE RULES. Remember, it is natural for your child to test the rules from time to time. Getting angry about such behavior only polarizes you and your child, and creates a family war that no one can win.

DON'T USE HARSH PUNISHMENT. When a child tests his parents, it is not helpful for him to be shown that his parents are bigger and stronger than he is by use of physical or verbal force. Punishment like this doesn't teach a child respect; it teaches him fear.

DON'T GIVE IN TO AN ARGUMENT. It is very tempting to give in to your child's wishes when you are tired and just want some peace and quiet. However, your child

can sense when you are feeling weak-willed; in fact, he often chooses that time to pressure you for what he wants. To avoid this trap, ask your child to quote the rule, taking the responsibility of remembering the rule off of you and putting it back on your child.

USE GRANDMA'S RULE. When your child yells and shows you disrespect, say in a calm voice, "When you speak to me in a respectful way, then you may do the things you like to do." (Also see GRANDMA'S RULE in "Discipline Dictionary.")

∿∿∿∿∿∿∿∿∿∿∿∿∿∿∿∿∿∿∿∿

Dissolving Disrespect

Carol Sylvester seemed to have been born to argue. Whenever her mother asked her to do something, Carol would implore, "I shouldn't have to work so hard. It's not fair! None of the other kids have to work all the time."

"Carol, stop arguing with me!" her mother would respond. "You don't do that much around here. You're nine years old and you should help around the house."

"I do work all the time and I'm not going to do it and you can't make me!" Carol would shout emphatically and head for her room.

Carol's mother realized she would always have this communication problem with her daughter until she began changing her responses to Carol's arguments.

"Why do I always have to help? Jennifer never has to do anything!" Carol wanted to know when her mother asked her to take out the trash one day.

"Carol, you seem to like to argue, and I'm tired of arguing," she began. "So I'm not going to argue with you anymore. When I ask you to do something, I'll give you five seconds to say you'll do it, and ten seconds after that to get started."

"That's dumb! Why do you have such dumb ideas?" Carol retorted.

"When you do as I ask," Mrs. Sylvester continued, ignoring her daughter's response, "then you will be allowed to do what you like. But if you refuse, or if you argue, I will give you extra jobs to do. Do you understand?"

"No, I don't understand, and I'm not going to do any jobs!" Carol retorted.

"Well, you have just earned one extra job," her mother calmly replied. "You will have to vacuum the living room now before you can do anything else."

At that point, Carol decided to have a tantrum. She screamed, stomped, and stormed to her room. When she showed up for dinner, she found her place had not been set.

"Where's my place?" she demanded.

"When you have finished your jobs, I'll warm your dinner and you may eat," her mother said matter-of-factly.

Carol, now somewhat subdued, hurriedly vacuumed the living room and took out the trash.

"Thank you for cooperating," her mother told her when she kissed her good night.

Carol didn't argue much after that—she had discovered there were many more rewards in cooperative behavior than in verbal combat.

Throwing Temper Tantrums

("I can't stand it when I can't go swimming. Just because I have an earache doesn't mean I can't go! I hate you!")

〰〰〰〰〰〰〰〰〰〰〰〰〰〰〰〰〰〰

Your childolescent has an uncanny ability to lose control when angry, frustrated, or disappointed. Why? She is attempting to control elements of her world that she cannot control. Because reason is blocked by anger, you cannot talk her into control. Instead, take yourself out of the wind of her anger until the gusts calm down and you can both listen quietly to each other. Then peacefully ask if she was disappointed, frustrated, or just plain hurt, and let her state her reasons for overreacting, no matter how unreasonable they seem to you.

Later, help her learn appropriate ways to exercise self-control. Show her that she can choose whether to behave angrily or not when faced with delayed gratification or disappointments.

Note: If your tantrumming child becomes violent and destructive, seek professional assistance in order to understand the roots of her anger and help her manage it.

PREVENTING THE PROBLEM

MODEL SELF-CONTROL. When you show your child how you cope with the frustrations in your life, she will be better able to develop her own self-control. Say, "I just had to get a new tire because I had a flat. There was nothing I could do about it, but I sure didn't like it."

EMPOWER YOUR CHILD. Giving your child a sense of power by presenting her with choices and allowing her to make decisions reduces the frustration that she may feel over not getting her own way. Say, "Let me tell you your choices. You can go to the party and have a good time or go and have a miserable time. You decide." A child who learns to make choices—even if it's a choice of attitude, such as, "I may not like to do art, but I can stand it!"—is less likely to use anger to get what she wants because she feels more in control of her life.

SOLVING THE PROBLEM

What to Do

TEACH ANGER MANAGEMENT. If your child has little self-control, teach her this direct anger-management strategy. Instruct her to slow down her anger by saying the words "smooth, calm, quiet, and soft" repeatedly while trying to feel the way the words suggest. Getting down on the floor and rolling up in a ball like a turtle will also help her feel more in control of her body, as well as her emotions.

Because it is really our thoughts about things that cause anger, not the things themselves, ask your child, "What were you thinking that made you so angry?" and help her to rearrange her thoughts so that she understands how not to upset herself over a situation.

Note: To ensure that your child is receptive to your lesson, teach these techniques during times of calm rather than times of anger.

IGNORE THE NOISE. Ignore your child's name-calling and verbal abuse by considering it as noise. When the noise passes, help your child to problem-solve without losing control. Say, "Now that you are calm, let's see if we can work out ways to deal with the problem that got you so angry." (See PROBLEM-SOLVING in the "Discipline Dictionary.")

ISOLATE TANTRUMS. When your child has a tantrum, it is important to isolate her. However, because six-to-twelve-year-olds are often difficult to move, physically, take *yourself* away from your tantrumming child. Go to a different part of the house and wait for the tantrum to end.

REWARD SELF-CONTROL. When your child does try to calm herself, lavish praise on her efforts in order to focus on the goal of self-control in a positive way. Give her attention for meeting this goal by saying, "Thank you for using self-control."

SET UP A TOKEN ECONOMY. If your child exercises self-control when she is angry and frustrated, encourage this healthy way of coping by offering her tokens that she can use to buy privileges. (See HOME TOKEN ECONOMY in the "Discipline Dictionary.")

What Not to Do

DON'T USE ANGER YOURSELF. It is impossible to convince your child to use self-control when you are frequently out of control.

DON'T IMPOSE HARSH PENALTIES OUT OF ANGER. Rather than correcting the situation, strong punishments, such as spanking or grounding, only encourage children to continue to be angry.

DON'T BE A HISTORIAN. After your child has grown calm, don't remind her of her past anger eruptions.

DON'T PAY OFF A TANTRUM BY GIVING IN TO YOUR CHILD'S DEMANDS OR BY GETTING UPSET.

The Eve of Destruction

Whenever six-year-old Eve didn't get to do, buy, or say whatever she wanted, she would explode with anger. When she was younger, she had such violent tantrums that Mr. Wally had begun to give in to her demands just to keep her from embarrassing him in public.

When Eve started getting angry at school, Mr. Wally knew that he had to do something about his daughter's behavior problem. She was alienating her friends, and her teacher was beginning to get upset because of her anger explosions.

"Mr. Wally," Eve's teacher began at a school conference, "Eve's temper is getting her into trouble at school. I would imagine that she has had problems with her temper at home, too."

"Oh, yes," Mr. Wally agreed, and he explained the problems that he had experienced with Eve.

Over the next hour, Eve's teacher outlined a plan that he thought might work—setting up a token economy at home so that Eve could earn tokens for anger control. They then called Eve into the conference and explained how the system worked.

First Eve was taught how to become a turtle when she felt angry—getting down on the floor and rolling up in a ball. While in this position, she was instructed to say, "Smooth, calm, quiet, and soft," over and over until she began to feel smooth, calm, quiet, and soft. Whenever she did that at home, she would be praised and paid tokens. She was instructed to use this turtling technique only at home in order to avoid being teased about it by her classmates.

During the next week at home, Eve's father frequently praised and paid tokens to Eve for her using her turtling technique. "Eve, you are using good self-control," Mr. Wally would say. And he would give her tokens that she could use to buy television-viewing time, something she dearly loved. After Eve was calm, he would also try to help her work out the problem that had made her so upset. "Now that you are calm, can you think of another way you could have handled my telling you that you couldn't have an ice cream bar?" Eve's father asked her.

"I could have asked politely?" Eve asked.

"But it was just before dinner!" her father answered.

"Then I could have waited until after dinner and had it for dessert," Eve volunteered brightly, as if making a new, important discovery.

"Good idea!" her father proudly replied.

As Eve began to get better at keeping her temper under control, her father also got better at resisting her demands. Eve seemed to like her newfound self-control, making both her school and home environments less turbulent places in which to grow.

Wanting Their Own Way

Never Being Satisfied

("I really, really need what I want
. . . now!")

∿∿∿∿∿∿∿∿∿∿∿∿∿∿∿∿∿∿∿∿∿∿∿∿∿∿

Too expensive? Too dangerous? Not appropriate? To childo-lescents, the fact that a privilege or purchase is too "any-thing" is not a good reason for them not to have or do what they say they can't live without having or doing.

Let this egocentric view of the world be your fair warning, because your child is just beginning to define his needs by what his peers have. These aren't really his needs, however, but are his wants. Making that distinction for yourself can guide your reaction to your child's excessive demands. And helping your child understand the difference between his wants and his needs is an essential first step before setting rules about how he can fulfill his wants.

Keep your values, budgets, and house rules in mind, as well, when your child begins to want what he wants when he wants it. Instead of punishing him for acting impatient and demanding, teach him the ways that he can obtain the items of his dreams (be that a baseball, wallet, or trip to the movies) just as you have learned the ways to get a new car or take a week-long vacation. This shifts the responsibility of obtaining privileges and possessions to your child.

PREVENTING THE PROBLEM

VALUE PEOPLE RATHER THAN THINGS. Establish an atmosphere in which your child is more likely to think about work and character, rather than possessions as the determinant of his worth. Comments, such as, "Did you see the Thomas's new BMW?" focus only on what a person owns. On the other hand, saying, "Wasn't that a wonderful thing Sally did when she volunteered her time to help some needy families?" focuses on Sally's behavior and the value it has. If your son sees behavior as an asset, he will be encouraged to behave appropriately.

LOVE YOUR CHILD FOR WHO HE IS. Giving unconditional love lets your child value himself and helps him put himself ahead of his possessions in importance. Unconditional love doesn't have expectations of others but rather accepts people as they are. Giving a child unconditional love means being able to give him a hug and a kiss even after he exhibits an inappropriate behavior. It says, "I'll always love you even though sometimes I may not like what you do."

GIVE YOUR CHILD OPPORTUNITIES TO CONTRIBUTE TO HIS FAMILY. Children who contribute to the functioning of their family through doing jobs and other family duties are more likely to develop family values and an attitude of selflessness. On the other hand, a child who isn't required to contribute to his family often becomes selfish and demanding because he isn't given the opportunity to see the value of his family over his possessions. Though initially your child may not enjoy doing chores, receiving praise from you about the completion of a job can help give him a sense of accomplishment.

TEACH YOUR CHILD HOW TO COMPROMISE. Rather than give in each time your child demands

something of you, get into the habit of offering him a compromise. For example, if you want to buy your son thirty-dollar tennis shoes, and he says that he "must have" fifty-six-dollar ones, tell him, "I will give you the amount of money to pay for the less-expensive shoes, and you can make up the difference with your own money." This approach communicates the double message that you are not going to automatically give your child anything he asks for and that he must make sacrifices to have what he wants.

PRAISE PATIENCE. Help your child learn how to be patient and get things in appropriate ways by pouring on the praise when he does.

SOLVING THE PROBLEM

What to Do

HAVE YOUR CHILD EARN WHAT HE GETS.
Instead of giving your child an allowance, set up an earning schedule for him, listing the chores that he is required to do weekly for which money is earned. This plan teaches your child the link between work and money. Establish three types of jobs in the family: Self-Help Jobs—those that keep your child going, such as making his bed, putting clothes in the hamper, and bathing; Family Jobs—those that keep the family going, such as setting the table, clearing the table, emptying the trash, and feeding the dog; and Contract Jobs—those for which money is paid, such as house-cleaning chores, yard chores, and chores for neighbors.

ENCOURAGE SAVING. A child who is taught to
save money and to use his savings to purchase highly desired items becomes much more appreciative of what he has. If your child wants a new radio, instead of rushing out to buy

it, suggest that he save up his earned money to buy it. Saving should not be mandated by a parent—it is a child's choice. But it is a good habit to *encourage*.

HAVE YOUR CHILD MATCH YOUR CONTRIBUTIONS.
When your child wants new clothing, offer to purchase the brand that you think is appropriate, style-wise, and is the best buy, financially. Then if he wants a more expensive brand, contract with him to make up the difference from his savings or earnings. This helps him make the purchasing decision based on how much having the jeans is worth to him.

GIVE GIFTS FREELY AND LOVINGLY.
Of course, you may give gifts to your child for special occasions, such as birthdays, or simply because you want to give him a gift. Overindulgence with gifts, however, can give him so many possessions that new ones become meaningless.

WHEN YOU GIVE YOUR CHILD GIFTS, GIVE THEM UNCONDITIONALLY.
In children's eyes, gifts often equal love. Therefore, when presents are given with strings ("I will give you this toy if you will share it with your brother") a child may believe that his parents' love is only given when he meets certain conditions.

BE FIRM.
Even though your child is having a full-blown temper tantrum and all the shoppers are staring at you because you will not let him buy a new shirt, don't give in to his demands just to quiet the storm. If you do, you will just be fueling his success rate and will be facing similar tantrums until you stop *your* behavior.

Instead, simply walk away and wait for the tirade to stop. Then discontinue the shopping trip (if possible) and, when you get home, levy the penalty of doing jobs. Say, "I'm sorry you chose to throw a tantrum; now you need to do a job for me."

SET CONSEQUENCES BEFORE GOING SHOPPING.

To avoid responding to your child's excessive demands, tell him what consequences his tantrums will bring. "Remember, if you choose to upset yourself about something while we're shopping, you are also choosing to do a job when we get home. The choice is up to you." Assigning jobs is a good consequence for your child's inappropriate behavior because by doing a job, your child is allowed to make up for his error by doing something constructive, thereby feeling good about himself at the same time.

What Not to Do

DON'T ARGUE WITH YOUR CHILD OVER HIS DEMANDS.

Remember that your child's goal in demanding his own way is to get control and attention. If you get into an argument with your child about his demands, he will have "won" your attention even if he "loses" the argument.

Rather than argue with your child about the demand, simply ask him for a restatement of the rule that you have previously established. Say, for example, "Yes, I understand that you say that you can't live without that coat, but what was the rule we made before we left?"

DON'T BECOME ANGRY.

When you become angry, you cannot think clearly, making you particularly vulnerable to your child, who may be determined to get what he wants. Talk to yourself in calming ways; say that it is only noise that your demanding child is exhibiting. Tell yourself that his noise will soon be replaced by quiet if you do not reinforce it by giving in to his demands.

DON'T GIVE YOUR CHILD THINGS ON DEMAND.

A child who learns by experience that he can quickly get anything he desires just by asking becomes unappreciative of what he has. Having your child earn what he gets or at least contribute to purchasing things teaches him a lesson about the relationship between working and reaching a goal.

DON'T FALL PREY TO PEER PRESSURE. If
you feel pressured to purchase things just because others have them, you are modeling the belief that "Things are more valued than people."

$\wedge$

Unappreciative Ellen

How can we help Ellen appreciate the zillions of things we buy and hours of effort we spend in trying to please her? That was the dilemma of Mr. and Mrs. Bunn in trying to manage their eleven-year-old's demanding attitude about life.

They reached their limit one day when Mrs. Bunn bought Ellen the special athletic shoes for which she had begged and whined. When they got home, Ellen told her mother that the shoes didn't look right—they were the wrong color and the strings were too long. She didn't really want them after all, she said, and she ended up wearing her old ones to school.

"You are so ungrateful!" Mrs. Bunn screamed.

"Well, it's your fault! You got the wrong ones!" Ellen stormed back.

That evening Mr. Bunn was told of the day's disaster; and he, too, became angry. After they had calmed down somewhat, they decided on a plan to help Ellen learn the value of the things she wanted. The next evening, they had a family meeting with Ellen to discuss the plan.

"Ellen, I'm sorry I got so upset and yelled at you about the shoes yesterday," Mrs. Bunn began. "But I'm afraid we've been doing the wrong thing by giving you everything you want. We have taught you how to be selfish."

"Do you mean you aren't going to get me anything any more?" Ellen inquired incredulously.

Mr. Bunn explained, "Here is how the plan will work. First, we will help you decide what you need. If you want something more than we decide, you can pay for the difference. If you need new jeans but want designer jeans, we'll pay for a pair of the regular jeans, and you can pay the difference to buy the designer brand."

"But I don't have any money. Where will I get the money to buy things I want? It's not fair. Other kids get what they want." Ellen shouted, pounding the table.

Mr. and Mrs. Bunn did not let Ellen's tantrum shake their confidence or demeanor. "See these index cards," Mrs. Bunn demonstrated. "We've written a job on each card and put an amount of money with it that we think the job is worth. When you need money, come see us and we'll give you some jobs to do to earn the money," she continued, ignoring Ellen's noise.

Later that week, Ellen asked for a neat little purse she had seen at the mall. "All the girls have them. Oh please, please, please!" she begged.

"Sure, you may buy one," Mrs. Bunn agreed, smiling. "I'll get the job cards. How much money do you need?" her mother asked.

"You mean I have to earn the money myself?" Ellen posed.

"Yes, that's what we decided. Remember?" her mother replied.

Ellen had another tantrum, but didn't get the purse . . . or the skirt, book, or necklace she wanted that week. Eventually, however, she got the picture. She began to work for what she wanted; and because she had to put out so much effort, she began to have a new feeling—appreciation of what her parents gave her.

Challenging Home Rules

("I don't need to follow rules I don't like!")

〜〜〜〜〜〜〜〜〜〜〜〜〜〜〜〜〜〜〜〜〜〜〜〜〜

Children of all ages need rules (often called "limits")—lines of demarcation between what they can and cannot do—in order to increase the predictability of and reduce the anxiety about their ever-widening worlds. If your child is regularly challenging your home rules, he is telling you that he wants more control over his own life. Challenging limits demonstrates a desire for self-sufficiency, which is a necessary beginning toward becoming independent. Empower your child in as many ways as possible, including involving him in the setting of limits. In addition, consistently enforce the consequences of his following and challenging the rules to teach him that rules are necessary and rewarding facts of life.

PREVENTING THE PROBLEM

SET RULES THAT ARE ENFORCEABLE. In order for a child to decide to follow rules, he needs to experience the benefits of doing so (such as getting to do what he wants). But keep in mind that the house rules to be followed while you are absent are not enforceable unless another adult is there to see that they are abided by. For example, setting a rule such as "no television-viewing after school" cannot be enforced because you have no evidence that your child did or did not follow the rule.

STATE RULES IN "TO DO" FORM. Telling a child what you want him to do rather than what you don't want him to do keeps him thinking positively and ensures that he is always aware of the behavior that you desire. Say, "The rule is: 'Get along with your brother,' " rather than, "The rule is: 'Don't fight!' " Initially, simply state the rules. When your child challenges them, develop a Rule Book that spells out all your house rules.

INVOLVE YOUR CHILD IN DEVELOPING THE RULES. A child is more likely to want to follow the rules if his help is enlisted in setting them. Say, "I think we need a rule about how far from home you can ride your bicycle." Then, when a rule has been created, ask, "What do you think the reward should be for following this rule? What should the consequences be for breaking it?"

PRAISE ADHERENCE TO THE RULES. Say, "Thank you for following the rule about getting along." A child who is frequently praised for following rules will be more likely to continue to do so.

KEEP RULES CONSISTENT. Help your child learn the different rules that need to be followed in church, at school, and at home so he can learn what to expect in different settings.

SOLVING THE PROBLEM

What to Do

REMAIN CALM. The fact that your child chooses to break a rule doesn't mean that he is becoming a criminal. By keeping cool and dealing with the rule violation in a consistent way, you will decrease the chances of having a shouting and screaming match between the guilty and law enforcement parties. Remember, getting angry and threatening your child does not teach him to follow rules—it only encourages him to sneak behind your back to commit crimes.

LET THE RULE STAND ALONE. Rules are statements of direction that can act as their own control. In the event that a rule is not being followed, the simple statement, "What's the rule?" can bring everyone back to the same neutral ground. It frees you from being the authority and allows you to work with your child so he may learn to follow the rule.

TEACH YOUR CHILD PROBLEM-SOLVING TECHNIQUES. View the breaking of a rule as a symptom of a problem for which a workable solution can be found. For example, view biting his brother as a symptom of your child's inability to cope with his brother's annoying behavior.

When your child violates a rule, the problem is how to get him to follow the rule. Ask, "What could you have done instead of breaking the rule about biting?" Then say, "I love you, but I don't like it when you test the rules. Remember, the rule is, 'We respect each family member's body.' " Finally, list the possible solutions that will help him keep the rule, such as ignoring his brother's behavior or walking away from his brother instead of biting him. Develop a final solution from the possibilities on this list.

SET UP INCENTIVE PLANS FOR RULE-FOLLOWING. Grandma's Rule is the easiest incentive to give children in order to encourage them to follow rules, particularly those rules for which they can see no logical reason. (See GRANDMA'S RULE in the "Discipline Dictionary.") Say, "When you have followed the rule about clearing away the dishes, then you may go play outside." A child will be more likely to choose to follow rules when his favorite activities are offered as rewards.

What Not to Do

DON'T YELL. When you yell at your child, you set up a mini-war in which the child becomes one armed camp and you become another. Children have little desire to follow the rules of the enemy!

DON'T THREATEN. When parents threaten a child, they invite him to rise to the challenge. Saying, "If you don't pick up your dirty clothes from your bedroom, then you won't go to Ron's," leads your child to test your willingness to carry out the threat. Instead, use Grandma's Rule, which states in a positive way the rule that needs to be followed and the reward for following it.

DON'T IMPOSE EXCESSIVE PENALTIES. When a child breaks a rule, he is telling his parents that they need to teach him how to follow the rule. Children don't learn from negative punishment; they learn best from their parents working with them to create incentives for rule-following.

DON'T BECOME THE RULE. You can easily become the rule by saying, "You will clean your room because I say so." This sort of statement allows your child to begin a battle of wills in which the rule itself gets lost. Parents can be manipulated; rules can't, unless parents choose to change them.

Playing by the Rules

Ten-year-old Tammy Tilson knew that following the rules was important when playing games with her friends. But she had learned long ago that if she pushed her Mom's rules with whining and tantrums, they would bend and sometimes break.

One day, her friend and she walked many blocks away from home to a convenience store to buy candy. Tammy knew that this not-so-quick trip was on her "forbidden" list; as expected, when Mrs. Tilson found out about it, she was angry enough to take firm action to end her daughter's lack of respect for rules.

Mrs. Tilson partly blamed herself for her daughter's behavior; she believed that she had created the problem by not strictly enforcing the rules in the past. So now she called Tammy in for a rule-making session.

"Tammy, we are going to have some new rules around here," Mrs. Tilson began. "First, we will make the rules together and keep them in a Rule Book so that we won't forget them. Second, we will make some consequences for the rules. For example, when you follow the rules, you will have more freedoms. When you don't follow the rules, you will receive more restrictions on what you can do." Tammy only smiled. She had been through this before, and she knew that after a while, things would be back to normal.

Soon Tammy broke a rule, one of the first to go into the Rule Book. The rule was: "When you leave your friend's house to go someplace else, you must call first to let me know where you are going." "I'm sorry you chose not to follow the rule when you left Suzie's to go to Jennifer's," Tammy's mother began. "By doing so, you also chose to lose the freedom to go to a friend's house for a week. I hope you can remember the rule next time you get to go to a friend's."

Tammy was beside herself. "It's not fair!" she shouted. But her mother didn't flinch. "These are stupid, dumb rules and I don't care if I ever get to go anyplace!" she screamed and rushed off to her room crying loudly. Tammy begged, pleaded, and threatened; but nothing changed the rule.

After a week of restriction, Tammy was once more allowed to go to a friend's. "Remember the rule," her mother said as Tammy was leaving, "and remember that for following the rule, you will get to go visit your friend's house as often as you like."

Tammy tested the rule once more, just to see if the old flexible mom would come back. But to her dismay, the rule and her mom stood the test. From that day on, Tammy followed the rules and reaped the rewards. Rules were good, she decided, because they always told her what to do in order to stay out of trouble.

Not Following Directions

("I don't have to do what I don't want to!")

〜〜〜〜〜〜〜〜〜〜〜〜〜〜〜〜〜〜〜〜〜〜〜〜

"I've told you a million times to go take a shower! How many times do I have to tell you?" Singing this rhetorical tune will only challenge your child to see how many times you will tell her to do something before you get serious about making her do it. To avoid this battle of wills, teach your child that following directions is the means to her end—getting to do what she wants. This helps her preserve her feelings of self-control and independence by allowing her to *choose* to do what you ask because she *wants* to earn her desired activity. By ignoring your child's retorts ("Make me!"), you can also keep the goal of compliance in your mind and not get derailed by her insolence.

PREVENTING THE PROBLEM

SHOW RESPECT FOR YOUR CHILD WHEN STATING DIRECTIONS.
Give your child the same respect that you would give a guest in your own home, saying "please" and "thank you" when appropriate. Everyone is more willing to comply when asked, rather than commanded, to do a task.

SET OBJECTIVES. Your child is more likely to follow directions if she has an understanding of the reasons why a task needs to be completed.

USE CONSISTENCY IN FOLLOWING UP. If your child knows that you won't check to see if a task has been completed, she is more likely to avoid following directions.

PRAISE YOUR CHILD AS SHE CARRIES OUT THE DIRECTIONS GIVEN. Your child is more likely to want to follow directions if her efforts are encouraged. Compliment her on those parts of a task which have been successfully completed and then ask her to finish the job.

SOLVING THE PROBLEM

What to Do

REMAIN CALM. When your child fails to follow directions, wait a minute or two before reacting. Calm yourself down, and plan how to achieve the goal of getting your child to do what you asked.

USE A STEP-BY-STEP STRATEGY. If your child is not in the habit of doing what she is told, teach her to do so by saying, "I love you, and I want you to learn how to follow directions." Tell her that she needs to answer, "Yes, I'll do it," before you can count to five; then she must begin the task before you count to ten; and finish the task within the time limit set.

GIVE ONE DIRECTION AT A TIME AND MAKE SURE THAT EACH TASK HAS BEEN

DONE BEFORE GIVING ANOTHER DIREC-TION.
Monitor how many directions your child can handle at one time. Only when she demonstrates that she is able to carry out more than one direction in succession should you give her two, three, or four at one time.

USE CHECKLISTS.
Don't expect your child to be able to remember all the things that she needs to be doing. Give her a checklist of the tasks for the day and the times the tasks need to be completed by. Then let her help decide on a time schedule to get the jobs done.

SET GOALS.
When goals are set for what your child needs to accomplish during the day and reasons are given for the goals, then she will be more likely to see how her work can give her a sense of accomplishment. Say, "When you have finished cleaning up the mess you made in the living room, then the house will be clean when Grandma arrives for her visit."

USE GRANDMA'S RULE.
By using this contract, you will help your child very quickly understand that her responsibilities must be carried out before her fun can begin. Say, "When you have cleaned your room, then you may go out and play."

What Not to Do

DON'T POINT OUT MISTAKES.
When a child is criticized for what she has not accomplished or not done correctly, she is less likely to want to do things when asked. Instead of being critical, simply say, "I like the way you did this part of the job. When you do the rest, then it will all be finished."

DON'T LABEL YOUR CHILD.
Children are often labeled as "lazy" when they don't want to do the things that

they are asked to do. However, the problem is rarely that a child is lazy but rather that she has not yet learned to be compliant. Grandma's Rule will help her learn that she will be rewarded for choosing to follow directions.

Acting Like a Big Shot

When John Alpert was told to empty the dishwasher and to take out the trash, it made him feel like such a "child." At the ripe old age of nine, he believed that he should be able to do what he wanted instead of taking orders from adults all the time.

"John, it's time to get the trash out and the dishes haven't been taken out of the dishwasher," Mrs. Alpert would inform him. "You know how you like to put it off until the last minute. Now, I want you to get started on it now! Tomorrow is the day for garbage pickup, and I want it done."

As his mother's words bounced around in his head, he said to himself, "I'm not going to take the trash out or empty the dishwasher, and she can't make me!"

When Mrs. Alpert arrived to see how John was doing with his assigned chores, she found the trash still piled by the door, the dishes weren't put away, and John was watching television.

"John, I thought I told you to get the trash out and empty the dishwasher," his mother began. "Why didn't you? You know they are your chores."

"Because I didn't want to, that's why!" John sharply retorted while wishing that his friends could see him in the midst of this open revolt.

But his mom only sat next to him on the sofa. "John, I know taking orders is tough sometimes, but the trash needs to be taken out today, and we need the clean dishes so we can have dinner tonight," Mrs. Alpert stated matter-of-factly. "We can't leave trash and garbage around the house all the time.

Before we know it, the house would be full, and we would be covered in bugs." John laughed at the image of his house that his mother kept so neat all the time being full of trash and bugs. "And besides, I need your help. We all need to work together to keep our family going.

"You have things you want to do, and I have things I want to do. Let's make a deal. You do the things I want, and I will help you get to do the things you want."

John only sat there, the remote control in his hand moving through the channels, as he appeared to ignore his mother.

"Now, you want to go over to Andy's this afternoon," Mrs. Alpert continued, "and I want you to be able to go. When the trash is out and the dishwasher is emptied, you may go. But because there is so much to do, I will help by supervising. Start by emptying the dishwasher. When that is done, then you can carry the trash out, and you will be finished. Tomorrow, I will make a checklist so that by following it, you can keep up with your chores on a daily basis so you won't have to listen to me remind you."

John sat for a few minutes mulling over the "deal" his mother had made with him. He reluctantly got up and went to the kitchen to begin his chores. His mother followed him. "You're doing a great job, John! It won't be long now. You must feel good about getting your jobs done so you can go to Andy's."

John did feel good, and he knew he was helping his family by doing his part. He and his mother hugged as she congratulated him after he had completed his jobs, then he hurried off to play with his friend.

Stubbornness

("I'm right no matter what!")

〰〰〰〰〰〰〰〰〰〰〰〰〰

When your ten-year-old son shouts that he *won't* make his bed or that he *must* wear shorts on a forty-degree day, he is really stubbornly refusing to give up control over himself, a power that he desperately wants (and needs). Give him that power by offering him choices (of what to wear, for example) with clearly stated consequences for each choice he makes. This allows him to practice decision-making and problem-solving on his own. In this way, you avoid casting your discussions in a right/wrong framework and you set up the make-a-choice rule as the authority, instead of you. In addition, the lesson that making decisions involves accepting the consequences of those decisions is one that will serve him as he moves into adolescence.

PREVENTING THE PROBLEM

CHANNEL STUBBORNNESS. Praise your child's stubborn behavior when it is appropriate—such as when he refuses to take a ride with a stranger—so that he will learn that it is okay to be stubborn in certain situations. This also rewards his ability to say no when others are pressuring him to do something he knows is dangerous or inappropriate.

TEACH YOURSELF HOW TO COMPROMISE. When you find yourself taking an absolute stand on an issue (telling your child, "No, I won't buy you a new skateboard."), try altering your position from an absolute stand to a compromise. Say, "I understand your position. But I have some concerns about buying this skateboard and I need to understand how you want to use it so we can see how to compromise about buying it." Then calmly discuss your concerns with your child to see if you can sort out these issues.

TEACH THE MEANING OF COMPROMISE.
Tell your child that a compromise happens when two people can't agree and they both give up a little of what they want so that each can have at least some of what they want.

PRAISE YOUR CHILD WHEN HE DOES SHOW THE ABILITY TO COMPROMISE. Say,
"That was a good compromise. Thank you for working hard at compromising."

SOLVING THE PROBLEM

What to Do

OFFER YOUR CHILD CHOICES. When offered
choices, your child can see that he does have some control over his destiny, which may keep him from getting into a power struggle with you. Say, "Here are your choices: You can do what I have asked and then be able to do what you want; or you can refuse to do what I've asked and then give up your playtime. You choose how you want to spend the day."

REWARD COMPROMISE. Offer your child rewards, such as praise, when he is willing to listen to your viewpoint and reach a compromise.

PUT ARGUMENTS ON HOLD. When faced with a child who is acting stubborn, it may be best to put the conflict on hold by getting away from each other. Say, "We aren't going to decide this now. We'll go do something else

for a while and talk about it later. Think through the issues, please, so we can discuss it more rationally when we get together." If your child refuses to put the discussion on hold, offer him choices. "You may do as I've asked and be able to play today, or you may fight with me and lose your privileges. You choose how you want it to be." Then isolate yourself (go to another part of the house) to avoid continuing the conflict.

SET UP A TOKEN ECONOMY. To increase your child's willingness to compromise on an issue, pay him tokens (to be turned in for privileges) each time he compromises. (See HOME TOKEN ECONOMY in the "Discipline Dictionary.")

What Not to Do

DON'T FALL INTO THE ANGER TRAP. When your child behaves stubbornly, you may find yourself getting angry. However, when you become angry, you declare war against your child. This only deepens his stubbornness and leads to continued conflict.

AVOID RIGHT/WRONG THINKING. When you find yourself thinking that you are absolutely right and your child is absolutely wrong, force yourself to see your child's point of view. Try to understand how he arrived at his position and then help him gather new information so that he, or you, can shift positions.

DON'T MAKE THREATS. Threats are intentions of action, but most threats of punishment that parents make are not carried out. Children learn quickly to ignore them because they are simply noise with no impact except on children's ears.

DON'T GET INTO A POWER STRUGGLE. Setting yourself nose to nose with your child only creates a war. Instead, enlist your child's cooperation by teaching him ways to cooperate.

DON'T LABEL YOUR CHILD "LAZY" OR "STUBBORN." Don't create a self-fulfilling prophecy by labeling your child "stubborn." A child who has been labeled may see the label as his destiny.

∧∧∧∧∧∧∧∧∧∧∧∧∧∧∧∧∧∧∧∧∧∧∧∧∧∧∧∧

The Preservation of Persistence

No matter what her mother requested, eleven-year-old Beth Anderson resisted. "You are so stubborn!" Mrs. Anderson would screech when they clashed over something, further motivating Beth to maintain her position. "I am not stubborn!" Beth would argue, substantiating her mother's claim.

Because she acted so obstinate, Beth also had difficulty getting along with her friends. No matter what they wanted to do, Beth would resist and hold out for her wishes. On the positive side, however, her ability to persist meant she didn't give up easily when faced with difficulty in her schoolwork or in anything else, for that matter.

"How can we help Beth act in less stubborn ways?" Mrs. Anderson asked her husband one evening after she'd had a particularly difficult day.

"Maybe some of the techniques I'm learning in the management courses I'm taking will help with Beth," he replied. After thinking about the problem for a few days, Mr. Anderson decided on a plan that would involve rewarding Beth for negotiation and compromise while allowing her to maintain her personal integrity.

"Beth, we have been concerned that we are always arguing with you and calling you 'stubborn,' and we don't like that," Mrs. Anderson explained the next night after dinner.

"We aren't always arguing!" Beth countered.

"We have a plan we'd like to tell you about that we think

will help us all get along better," Mr. Anderson stated. "The plan will start with a token economy. We will pay tokens for your cooperating with our requests. When we ask you to do something, we will pay tokens if you answer yes within five seconds. Then we will pay you again if you can get started in ten seconds, and finally we will pay you again if you can finish meeting the request in a reasonable amount of time."

"I'm not going to do this. This is stupid!" Beth repeated in disgust.

"The tokens you earn will be used to buy time doing the things you like to do, such as having friends over to play, watching television, or arguing with us about things," Mr. Anderson continued, ignoring Beth's editorializing.

"You mean I have to pay for those things now?" Beth asked.

"Yes. That's the way the plan works. I'm sure you'll like it after a while," her father said, and he continued describing the plan. "If you feel things aren't fair, you may negotiate with us about it. All you have to do is ask permission to talk to us about the problem and then make a proposal about how you would like the problem to be solved."

Immediately after the plan was instituted, Beth didn't earn many tokens. But soon she found that being deprived of the things she enjoyed doing increased her desire to be more compliant. Earning tokens was actually fun, as was negotiating with her parents because of the sense of power that negotiating gave her. Within several weeks, Beth became less stubborn but was still persistent in getting things done—exactly the balance her parents had tried to reach in how this trait of hers was displayed.

Demanding Freedom

("Why can't I go wherever I want to go whenever I want to?")

∿∿∿∿∿∿∿∿∿∿∿∿∿∿∿∿∿∿∿∿∿∿∿∿∿

How much is too much and how little is too little? That is the question plaguing most parents when it comes to deciding how much freedom to grant their middle-years children.

You want to avoid raising a rebel who knows no limits because none have ever been provided (and enforced). Examine your child's history of accepting responsibilities before doling out greater freedoms and privileges. Ask yourself if your child comes home when you call her. Has she called from a friend's house when she's ridden her bike there, as you asked her to do? Does she follow directions when you tell her that she can only go to one friend's house and not roam the neighborhood?

If the answer to the above questions are No, then teach your child how to handle her freedom responsibly as she proves herself worthy of being on a boundary-expansion program. Before you can grant her the freedom to travel to virgin territories, she needs to demonstrate to you that she has learned the skills she will need to deal with problems that may arise.

PREVENTING THE PROBLEM

ALLOW DEVELOPMENTALLY APPROPRIATE FREEDOMS. A child who learns in the middle years to accept freedom and its attendant responsibilities (such as being able to ride her bicycle to a friend's, but having to call when she arrives) will be more likely to handle freedom responsibly later. Holding a child too close (not letting her play with friends or try new ventures that are safe) only retards her growth and ability to handle childhood experiences.

PRAISE APPROPRIATE USE OF FREEDOM.
A child who demonstrates her ability to handle independent activities appropriately should have her behavior praised. This encourages her to continue to use freedom wisely and avoid violating the rules that can get her into trouble.

COMMUNICATE TRUST. A child who believes she
is trusted is less likely to violate that trust. When your child wants to walk home after school, and you believe that she can, say to your child, "I know I can trust you to walk straight home after school, so I will allow you to walk instead of ride the bus." This sets the child up to meet the challenge of trust.

SOLVING THE PROBLEM

What to Do

NEGOTIATE LIMITS. When your child demands more
freedom than you are willing to give her, try negotiating a compromise. Involve her in cooperative goal-setting, so she will be more likely to follow the rules. If she asks for two hours of free, unsupervised time after school, offer her a half hour of that time with the goal of increasing it to an hour, then an hour and a half, etcetera, as she acts responsibly for each time period.

SET DEFINITE LIMITS. When your child demands and
gets more freedom, make sure that the freedom comes with

specific limits. Say, "Yes, you may play with your friends, but I must know where you are. You must call me when you get to your friend's house and let me know that you have arrived there." This way, you will stay informed of your child's whereabouts and will be able to know if your child can be trusted to follow the rules. Your child will feel more secure, too, knowing what she may and may not do.

PRAISE COMPLIANCE. When a new freedom has been given and a challenge has been met successfully, praise your child's effort. Say, "Thank you for calling me when you got to Sally's. That was very responsible of you." This specific praise increases the chance that your child will follow rules in the future.

USE CONSEQUENCES FOR RULE VIOLATIONS. If your child abuses a new freedom, take that freedom away for a specific period of time, then give her another chance to show she has learned from the restriction. Say, "I'm sorry that the rule about riding your bicycle on our busy street wasn't followed. That will mean that you will not be able to ride your bicycle for a week. Then, we will try again next week. When you've shown that you can follow the rule, you can have the privilege back." The loss of a privilege is a natural way of reminding a child of the rule she has violated.

What Not to Do

DON'T OVERREACT WHEN NEW FREEDOMS ARE ABUSED. When your child does things without permission, such as go to a friend's house without asking, your overreacting by imposing severe punishment (such as grounding or spanking) will not make her act more responsibly in the future. Rather, it will encourage her to be sneaky and devise ways to avoid getting caught.

DON'T GIVE TOO MUCH FREEDOM TOO SOON.

A child who is given more freedom than she can handle responsibly often feels a lack of support from her parents, though she would never admit it. Carefully monitor how well a certain freedom is accepted before deciding whether you should continue to allow the freedom or withdraw it.

The Oxler Strings Saga

Eleven-year-old Megan Oxler wanted to go to the shopping mall on Saturday and spend the day hanging out. She then wanted to go to an evening movie and be picked up around nine at night. Her mother wasn't sure how to react to this request. Should a fifth grader be allowed to cruise the mall, she wondered.

"Oh, Mom, please let me go to the mall!" Megan pleaded. "All the other kids get to go, and I'm the only one who doesn't. They all think I'm a baby because I can't do everything!"

"I don't feel comfortable letting you go to the mall for the day," her mother countered.

"But everybody gets to go. I'm the only one who doesn't," Megan wailed.

"Megan, I'm going to call Alicia Rossi's mother," Mrs. Oxler stated in order to buy some time before making her decision. She also wanted to collect the facts. "You and Alicia have been best friends forever, and I doubt if Mrs. Rossi is letting her go to the mall each Saturday."

"I'm so glad you called," Mrs. Rossi said when Megan's mother phoned. "Alicia has been telling me the same thing that Megan's been telling you. She says that everybody else is getting to go. Well, I called Mrs. Washington, Tanya's mother, and she had the same story."

"Maybe we all need to get together and decide what we're going to allow these girls to do and what we aren't. Otherwise, they'll make us think that they are really being deprived." Megan's mother laughed.

The mothers decided that the girls could go to the mall for two hours on Saturday afternoon and then, if they wanted to go to a movie, one of the parents would accompany them back to the theater that evening. The girls could then have some of the freedom they wanted, but within limits.

"Oh, Mother, that's so stupid!" Megan stormed after hearing of the new rules.

"Well, those are the rules, dear. I guess you can take what you have been offered, or you can not go at all. You decide how you want it to be," she calmly offered.

Megan decided to take the offer; however, she and her friends found after a few trips to the mall that it was actually boring to go there. They had made it out to be such a big deal when they talked about it with each other that it could never have lived up to its billing; but they had to experience this lesson firsthand to learn it. Doing so within appropriate boundaries helped them feel secure while they safely let go of a little more of their parents' apron strings.

Irresponsibility/
Disorganization

Messiness and Shirking Home Responsibilities

("I don't care if my jobs are done!")

〜〜〜〜〜〜〜〜〜〜〜〜〜〜〜〜〜〜〜〜〜〜〜〜〜

If the members of the younger generation in your house rely on you to clean up their messes, this undemocratic state of affairs needs to be tackled. Don't assume that young folks cannot accomplish chores as effectively as you. Instead, make your child self-reliant when it comes to doing home clean-up routines. Teach him that everyone in the family must participate in helping the home run smoothly by establishing the rule that activities that used to be unearned privileges are now earned ones—granted only when chores are completed.

PREVENTING THE PROBLEM

SET REASONABLE GOALS. Determine the physical capabilities of your child as you involve him in deciding what his home chores will be.

HELP YOUR CHILD UNDERSTAND HIS ROLE AS HELPER. A child who sees himself as a valuable contributor to the family feels good about himself and the work he is doing. "Each job is just as important as another" is a critical message to communicate to your child when doling out family responsibilities. By not trying to make chores "equal," you will avoid giving your child the expectation that fairness must exist on the issue of home jobs.

MODEL TIDINESS. A child who sees his parents leaving little messes around the house—empty drinking glasses by the television, dirty dishes on the kitchen table, and unmade beds—finds it more difficult to understand why he must follow rules requiring *him* to pick up after himself.

PRAISE CLEANLINESS. When your child remembers to return his empty glass to the kitchen, praise him for his effort. Saying, "Thank you for remembering to put your dirty glass in the dishwasher. That is so helpful!" encourages your child to continue the practice.

ESTABLISH A ROUTINE OF KEEPING THINGS CLEAN. When a child understands that cleanliness is expected of him, he is more likely to establish habits of picking up after himself. Make cleaning-up routines part of daily life, not only part of the consequences for inappropriate behavior.

KEEP BELONGINGS USEFUL. Regularly clean out old items (such as clothes, toys, etcetera) that are not being used in order to reduce the clutter around your house.

USE CHECKLISTS. When a checklist of things to do around the house is the boss—the control over what gets done—you can be the support system to praise your child's efforts. Set up the checklist according to the order in which things are to be done. On a "Things to Do Before School" list, include getting up, making your bed, getting dressed, and eating breakfast. This sequence will seem logical to your child because it uses the natural consequence of breakfast as a reward for completion of the first three items.

PRAISE YOUR CHILD'S BEHAVIOR WHEN HE MEETS HIS RESPONSIBILITIES. Children

like to have recognition for a job well done. Praise not only encourages your child to continue meeting his responsibilities, but gives him a sense of accomplishment and a feeling of belonging to the family.

SOLVING THE PROBLEM

What to Do

USE THE "SATURDAY BOX." When your child leaves his personal belongings lying around creating clutter, pick up the items he has abandoned and put them in the "Saturday Box" (a closet or chest which can be locked). On Saturday, return those items to your child with a job assigned to each commodity. Say, for example, "I'm sorry you left your jacket in the hall, Steve. Here it is and here is the job you must do to make up for leaving it where it didn't belong."

SET CLEAN-UP RULES. Establish clean-up rules so that your child understands what you expect him to do. "You must put toys away before getting out something else to play with" and "You must put your dirty dishes in the dishwasher when you are finished with them" are two examples of rules that clearly state the jobs to do.

USE OVERCLEANING. Cleaning up after himself, followed by cleaning up something else, teaches a child the importance of tidiness and gives him ownership of the areas he has cleaned. His putting effort into making things tidy not only helps him understand how to go about making things clean, but also makes his keeping that space clean very important to him. Tell your child, "I'm sorry that you left an empty glass by the television. Now you must put it where it belongs, and then vacuum and dust the room in which you left it."

WHEN MESSINESS STRIKES, USE A CHECKLIST.
When your child lapses into messiness habits, create a checklist of clean-up routines to remind him of your cleanliness expectations. Say, "You need a checklist to remind you of what you need to do. When you complete the items on that list, then you may do what you would like to do."

FOCUS YOUR ATTENTION ON WHAT HAS BEEN DONE.
When a child fails to live up to his responsibilities, lavish praise on what he did accomplish. Your child will respond better if you point out his accomplishments rather than what he failed to do. Say, "I like the way you cleaned off your bed. When the floor and desk are cleaned, the whole room will be done."

SEPARATE YOUR CHILD FROM HIS BEHAVIOR.
If your child is not meeting his responsibilities, say, "I love you, but I do not like your not doing your assigned chores around the house."

USE GRANDMA'S RULE.
Say, "When you have done the things on your checklist, then you can go out and play with your friends." This statement tells your child what has to be done and what rewards he will receive for doing those things.

What Not to Do

DON'T LABEL YOUR CHILD.
A child who doesn't fulfill his responsibilities is often called "lazy." He isn't lazy; he just hasn't gained a sense of responsibility and needs to be taught how to accomplish his home duties.

DON'T OVERLOAD YOUR CHILD. Often a child is asked to be responsible for tasks that are not age-appropriate, or he is asked to be responsible for more tasks than he can handle.

DON'T NAG ABOUT MESSINESS. Nagging only makes people angry and resentful, and doesn't help a child learn how to clean up after himself. Nagging also makes a child dependent on being reminded to do things by his parents.

DON'T GIVE HARSH PENALTIES FOR LAPSES IN MESSINESS. A child doesn't learn how to follow clean-up rules from being given harsh penalties; he only learns how to be punished.

DON'T MAKE YOURSELF ANGRY. When your child doesn't remember to pick up after himself, you may feel angry and unappreciated. Rather than get into an angry mood, simply remember that your child's agenda and yours do not always match—and that your child needs to be taught how to follow yours.

DON'T EXPECT PERFECTION. Don't expect jobs to be done as you would have done them. Remember, perfection is an unattainable goal.

Off-Duty Dan

Seven-year-old Dan Misemer could find a thousand things to do that were more interesting than the chores his mother assigned to him. Instead of making his bed, he built airplanes with his lock-blocks. Instead of carrying out the trash, he watched television.

"Dan, you didn't make your bed again this morning before

school," his mother would tell him. "How many times must I tell you to make your bed?" his mother would lament.

"I don't know," Dan would answer aimlessly. He really didn't know what the fuss was all about. He would only be messing up his bed again that night, so he didn't care if it was made or not.

Eventually, Dan's parents held a family meeting to decide what to do about their son's shirking of his chores. First they reviewed his list of daily chores. For a seven-year-old, he was not overburdened, they thought. Next, they made a checklist of Dan's chores, listing them in logical sequence.

The next day, they presented Dan with the checklist, saying, "Dan, this is to help you remember to do your chores. To help you want to do them, we have decided on a new rule: When you have done your chores, just check them off the list, and then come tell one of us. We'll inspect the job to make sure it's finished. Then you will be free to do what you want to do."

"Do you mean I can't play outside after school until these chores are done?" Dan asked, incredulous over this new state of affairs. "That's what it says here on this dumb checklist."

"That's right, Dan. When you have done the chores, then you get to play," his mother replied warmly, but emphatically. "We understand that you don't like this list, but the rule stands. When you want to play with your friends after school, watch television, or do anything you want to, the chores have to be done first."

Dan stomped out and spent almost two hours in his room. He would open his door from time to time and shout his defiance at his parents, then slam the door shut, but they resolved to stand firm.

Eventually, Dan began doing his chores and even became cheerful as he followed his checklist because, by doing so he got to do what *he* wanted to do. His parents rejoiced, too, not only because Dan was now acting responsibly, but also because they had been strong enough to wait out his tantrum and stand by the rule they had established.

Forgetfulness

("I didn't bring my math assignment home, and I don't remember where I put my math book.")

∧∧∧∧∧∧∧∧∧∧∧∧∧∧∧∧∧∧∧∧∧∧∧∧∧∧∧∧

Because your child's priorities are different from yours, when there are chores to be done, books to be brought home, and jackets to be accounted for, tasks and belongings are easily forgotten. To melt your child's cries of "I forgot" into cheers of "I remembered!" give her practice in following instructions and praise her behavior when she remembers what she has to do. Become more organized—by creating specific places for specific things, for example—to help your child structure her life and turn forgetful behavior from a habit into only an occasional problem.

Note: If your child loses and forgets things chronically, to a degree where her self-confidence is affected ("I'll never remember anything," she begins saying), she may have a learning disability called "Attention-Deficit Disorder." The disability has many characteristics, including difficulty in focusing attention on activities that aren't of high interest. It may also affect a child's ability to follow directions and complete tasks at home and at school. Attention-Deficit Disorder is a learning disability that requires diagnosis by a qualified specialist, generally a psychologist. If you suspect your child has this problem, contact her school or physician for a referral to a specialist.

PREVENTING THE PROBLEM

PROVIDE A TIGHT STRUCTURE. A child who
easily forgets things may have too much on her mind for her
to be internally organized, so she needs a good external structure. Making "to do" lists for your child is a way of providing
her with an extra sense of security about being able to do
what needs to be done. The list can tell her what chores she
has to do and when they are to be completed, reducing the
need for you to be with your child at all times as the reminder.

MODEL WAYS OF REMEMBERING. When you
show your child through your own behavior how to use memory aides such as lists and notes, your child will have a better
idea of how to go about helping herself remember things. If
you forget to do something, show your child how you will try
to prevent forgetful behavior in the future. Say, "I forgot to
pick up the clothes at the cleaners! I need to make myself a
note and put it where I will see it so I don't forget tomorrow."

SET RULES FOR WHERE THINGS BELONG.
A child who forgets where she puts things generally doesn't
have set places where things belong. Teach your child how
to keep herself more organized. Tell her, "I have cleaned off
a shelf in this closet for your volleyball equipment. The rule
is: 'You are to put all your volleyball things on the shelf when
you have finished with them so you will know where they are
when you want them again.' "

SOLVING THE PROBLEM

What to Do

USE GRANDMA'S RULE. Encourage your child to become more organized by stating the consequences of her reaching this goal. Say, for instance, "When you have completed the items on your 'to do' list, you may play a game." (See GRANDMA'S RULE in the "Discipline Dictionary.") Also, rather than constantly reminding her about the list, ask your child to bring it to you for periodic verification of chore completion.

PRAISE ORGANIZATION AND MEMORY. When your child remembers to do what she is told and organizes herself in even the smallest way, call it to her attention. Say, "Thank you for remembering to bring your spelling book home. How did you help yourself remember?" This not only praises your child's behavior but also helps her review her strategies for remembering.

MAKE SURE THAT YOUR CHILD FOLLOWS THROUGH WITH INSTRUCTIONS. Don't let your child use poor memory to get out of doing what she is told; allowing excuses only encourages the problem. When you tell her to do something, count to five. Before you reach five, she is required to answer, "Okay, I'll do it." Then count to ten. During the one-to-ten count, she is required to begin the task. Set a timer for when the task must be completed. After it is done, praise her follow-through.

FOCUS ON REMEMBERING. A child often resorts to putting herself down when she constantly forgets. Saying, "I'm so dumb!" may be her response to having forgotten to bring her spelling book home. Rather than get caught up in your child's self-criticism, focus her attention on how to prevent the problem the next time. Ask her, "How can you remember to bring your book home tomorrow?" If she can't come up with any solutions, suggest, "Perhaps putting it in your backpack right after you use it in class tomorrow will help you remember it."

What Not to Do

DON'T COME TO THE RESCUE. If you run to school to take her lunch to her every time she forgets it, or if you pay for the book every time she loses one from the library, your child will miss opportunities to learn how to solve her problems of losing and forgetting.

DON'T GET ANGRY. A child who forgets or who loses things may not have learned how to be organized. Your anger simply makes your child feel bad about herself. Instead of losing control of your emotions, teach your child what she can do to help herself be better organized.

DON'T PUT YOUR CHILD DOWN. When your child continues to forget things, you may become so frustrated that you are tempted to shout, "Why can't you remember anything?" This statement has no logical answer, of course, because if your child knew how to remember, then she wouldn't be forgetting. Instead of putting your child down, be supportive of her and help her develop ways of remembering.

Why Larry's Not a Loser

Larry Beeson would lose his head if it weren't fastened on. At least that's what his mother often said to him as he searched for something that he had lost. Larry tried to keep track of his things; but at the age of ten, there always seemed to be other things to think about.

"Larry, we need to do something about your forgetfulness," Mr. Beeson said to his son one afternoon. "You forget to bring your homework home from school, you lose your assignments and your shoes, and last week you lost the new baseball glove that you got for your birthday!"

"But I found the glove," Larry protested. "It was at Joe's house. He brought it to me yesterday."

"I know, but you often have trouble remembering to do things and remembering where you put things," Mr. Beeson stated. "I spoke to your teacher yesterday, and she agrees. So we have worked out a plan to try to help you remember things. First, your mother and I have made up this checklist for you. It includes all the things that you need to remember to do before you go to school. Beside each thing is the number of points you will earn for remembering," his father explained as Larry's attention began to wander.

"Larry, please pay attention," Mr. Beeson began. "Here's another checklist for school. On it are the things that you have to remember to do at school before you come home from school. All you need to do is check off the things as you do them."

"What was that, Dad?" Larry suddenly asked, as if he had just returned from a long mental trip.

His father patiently explained the use of the checklist again. He knew that this would help to some extent, but he also was aware that Larry might have a problem with remembering things because he, too, had such a problem. Luckily, he had learned many tricks to help himself with his poor memory that he was eager to pass on to his son.

Sleeping/ Eating/Hygiene Problems

‹‹‹

Resisting Bedtime

("If I go to bed, I may miss something!")

∧∧∧∧∧∧∧∧∧∧∧∧∧∧∧∧∧∧∧∧∧∧∧∧∧∧∧∧∧∧∧

Your child may now be able to stay awake long after you've conked out on the couch, but don't be fooled into thinking that he should be allowed to change his nightly bedtime hour as he sees fit. Remember that you know the amount of sleep that your child needs in order for him to feel his finest when the rooster crows. Establish a reasonable hour for him to be in bed, then use the game Beat the Clock to enforce bedtime so that you can play a supportive role in helping him get ready for bed, instead of being thought of as the "bedtime bad guy."

PREVENTING THE PROBLEM

DECIDE WHAT IS AN APPROPRIATE BEDTIME FOR YOUR CHILD, BUT REMEMBER TO BE FLEXIBLE. Keep in mind that the actual time that a child needs to be tucked in will change as he grows and as daily activities change. Establish different bedtimes for summer, vacations, and special occasions (such as holidays) to prevent confusion over when to enforce and when not to enforce a certain bedtime hour.

MAKE THE END OF THE DAY A POSITIVE TIME. A child loves to share his day with his parents, so allow time before bed for talking about the major events of the day, for problem-solving, and for simply sharing feelings. This can prevent your child from needing to fight at bedtime to get your attention.

MAKE EXERCISE A DAILY HABIT. A child who gets an appropriate amount of exercise every day usually tumbles to bed exhausted.

KEEP BEDTIME AS CONSISTENT AS POSSIBLE. Busy schedules don't always allow for a consistent bedtime, but try to maintain a reasonable time for sleep so that going to bed is a habit rather than a surprise.

AVOID LATE-NIGHT EMERGENCIES AND SURPRISES. Set up a rule about doing homework early in the evening so that your child is not worried about undone activities at bedtime. If an assignment slips by, getting up earlier the next day to complete the task may be preferable to your child's trying to do it at the end of the day when he is tired.

SET ASIDE PART OF YOUR EVENING FOR PLAYING, READING, TALKING, AND SIMPLY BEING CLOSE TO YOUR CHILD.

SOLVING THE PROBLEM

What to Do

PLAY BEAT THE CLOCK. To solve the problems of bedtime hassles, follow this routine using a sixty-minute kitchen timer as the bedtime reminder. Here's how it works:

- An hour before the time your child should be in bed, set the timer for five minutes and say, "When the timer rings, it will be time to start getting ready for bed."
- When the timer rings, say, "The timer says that it is time to start getting ready for bed. When you beat the timer, you will get to stay up and read and talk for a while." Set

the timer for a reasonable amount of time to allow your child to bathe and/or get into his pajamas (about five to fifteen minutes).

■ While the timer is motivating your child to hurry getting ready, your role is to praise your child for the effort he is making to get ready for bed before the timer rings.

■ When your child beats the timer, he may stay up to talk with you, read, or play for the remaining time within the hour originally established as the "going to bed" hour. If he doesn't, he must go to bed immediately.

USE GRANDMA'S RULE. Say, "When you get ready for bed by a certain time, then you have these privileges. If you choose not to, then here are the consequences." Privileges could include getting to read or play in bed, or getting to play after school—in other words, afternoon or evening privileges. Consequences include having to go to bed earlier the next night or losing an evening privilege.

KEEP THE ORDER OF EVENTS OF THE BEDTIME ROUTINE, EVEN IF THE TASKS ARE DONE LATER THAN USUAL. Bedtimes may vary on weekends, holidays, and summers, but if for some reason a bedtime routine can't be kept at its usual time, maintain the routine and shorten the time in which it is done. A child likes the predictable nature of routine, and will be less likely to engage in a bedtime battle if the routine is followed with as few exceptions as possible.

What Not to Do

DON'T LET YOUR CHILD CONTROL BEDTIME. An older child may be allowed to negotiate for a reasonable bedtime; but once the time has been set, it must be strictly followed. Inconsistent enforcement only tells a child that he can try to negotiate bedtime every night. (See NEGOTIATION in the "Discipline Dictionary.")

DON'T THREATEN AT BEDTIME. Threats are only effective on a short-term basis. Rely instead on the consequences built into the routine (having to go directly to bed without any extra playtime) to motivate your child to get to bed on time.

DON'T MAKE BEDTIME A MAJOR BATTLE. Fighting with your child every night at bedtime creates an unpleasant atmosphere, which prevents sleep rather than encourages it.

DON'T ALLOW TELEVISION-VIEWING FOR LONG PERIODS AFTER SCHOOL. Encourage bike riding and other outdoor activities to promote your child's physical well-being.

Midnight Madness

Bedtime had always been hassle time for Mr. and Mrs. Graverson. They would start getting their children, Bart and Betty, ready for bed at an early hour; but by the time the task was accomplished, the children were crying, the adults were exhausted, and the clock had rolled on way past the time that the youngsters should have been in bed.

When the children turned seven and nine years old, respectively, their parents designed a bedtime plan to last an hour and to be controlled by a timer. One night, an hour before bedtime, they began to explain the new rules of the plan: "I set a timer for five minutes," Mrs. Graverson said. "When the timer rings, it will be time to start getting ready for bed."

The children continued to play as if they had not heard what their mother had said. When the timer rang, they were told, "The timer says it's time to start getting ready for bed. Now let's reset the timer and see if you can beat the clock by getting yourself ready for bed before the timer rings again.

Whoever beats the timer will be allowed to stay up and play for a while." The timer was reset and suddenly the children were moving.

"You are really hurrying. You're going to beat the timer and get to stay up and play!" Mrs. Graverson encouraged. Sure enough, both children beat the timer and were able to stay up and play. The timer was then reset, so that they would know when it was time to get into bed.

"The timer says it's time to brush teeth and get into bed," the children's parents announced when the timer rang again. "Whoever beats the timer gets to read in bed for a while."

Both children hurried as they brushed their teeth. Because they beat the timer once again, they were allowed five minutes' reading time after they said their good nights to their parents.

At the final timer, the parents announced, "Timer says lights out. Whoever turns off the light and is quiet will get to stay up tomorrow night and play just like we did tonight."

Both lights went out immediately. "Good night. We love you," the happy parents called out, grateful that they had found the switch to put the lights out on their children's bedtime hassles, too.

Poor Eating Habits

("I can eat whatever I want!")

〜〜〜〜〜〜〜〜〜〜〜〜〜〜〜〜〜

If your child will only eat peanut butter for dinner, don't stock up on economy-size jars. Food fetishes (like eating only one food, not eating, and overeating) are ways that some childolescents test their parents' authority. These children get rewarded for their food fetishes by seeing how much they upset their parents.

Consider whether your child is exercising power through food because you are limiting her decision-making power in other areas of her life. Take away the attention that your child gets for practicing poor food habits and replace it with a rule: You provide the food and your child decides whether or not she will eat it.

Include your child in meal planning and preparation; discuss nutrition with her and let her make dietary decisions. This helps her learn how to make appropriate food choices, too.

Note: Because your child's diet can put her health in immediate jeopardy and set the stage for future eating disorders, monitor her inability to delay gratification or her obsession with losing weight. If you are concerned that your child may have an eating disorder, contact a competent counselor at a clinic or hospital that has a specialized eating disorders program.

PREVENTING THE PROBLEM

BUY HEALTHY. You can control what foods you have at home. Eliminate purchasing those that compromise your family's health.

MODEL GOOD EATING HABITS. Watching you eat proper foods will set the stage for your child's knowing how to follow a proper diet. Not only should you model the eating of appropriate foods at meals, but you should restrict your own intake of junk food.

ESTABLISH A DINNER HOUR FOR THE FAMILY. During the family dinner hour, make conversation—not television—the entertainment. Conversing encourages slower eating and allows the family to be more aware of how much is being eaten. Watching television while eating also establishes a habit of thinking about food whenever the television is blaring.

SOLVING THE PROBLEM

What to Do

HELP YOUR CHILD ESTABLISH HEALTHY EATING HABITS. Eliminate junk foods from the house or lock them away. Provide vegetables and fruit for snack foods. If your child is an overeater, make all foods legal, reduce the size of her portions, don't give her second helpings, and encourage her to put her fork down between bites.

ENCOURAGE EXERCISE. Children who are overweight generally don't eat more than those who are of normal weight; they simply don't exercise as much. Rather than driving your child to her friend's house, encourage her to walk or ride her bike if the route is a reasonable distance and is safe. Encourage her to become involved in sports activities and take her along on your own walks, bicycle rides, or jogs.

MAKE A SCHOOL RULE ABOUT SHARING FOOD. Encourage your child's school to make a rule about sharing food during lunch period to ensure that your child has an appropriate amount of food. If your child breaks the rule by taking food from other children's plates, her lunchroom supervisor or the school nurse may enforce whatever consequence the school had established for breaking this rule, such as requiring a child to eat at a separate table from her classmates at her next lunch period.

What Not to Do

DON'T MAKE A FUSS ABOUT FOOD. If you focus on your child's eating habits, she may be encouraged to use food as a tool to get attention. If she doesn't want to eat a particular meal, simply cover the plate with plastic wrap and make it available when she is hungry.

DON'T FORCE YOUR CHILD TO EAT WHEN SHE SAYS SHE ISN'T HUNGRY. Your child may not always feel hungry when a meal is served. Forcing her to eat at that time will only teach her to eat when she isn't hungry. In addition, it may encourage her to respond to emotional cues instead of hunger cues. If your child refuses a meal, wrap it, refrigerate it, and give it to her later.

Note: Be aware of other causes of not eating, such as depression, too much snacking, anorexia nervosa, or physical illness. Consult your pediatrician if your child continuously says she's not hungry at mealtime.

DON'T FORCE YOUR CHILD TO EAT AFTER SHE IS FULL. The cry of the nurturing parent—"Make a happy plate!"—teaches a child to eat even after she feels full. If a child has only picked at her food and claims to be full, wrap it, refrigerate it, and bring it out later when she is hungry.

AVOID CONSTANT TALK OF DIETING. A
child who hears parents talking of diets all the time begins to
think she will be valued only if she also loses weight. A child
should never restrict her calories or alter dietary intake dramat-
ically without medical supervision. Dieting can be especially
harmful to a child when it robs her of essential nutrients.

DON'T EAT ALL OVER THE HOUSE. Children
and adults should eat only in the areas of the house designated
for eating so that the meal and the company are the focus of
attention, not the television or other activities.

Dying to Be Thin

Tabi Butcher was a healthy, athletic girl who had always had
a lot of friends. But when she was in the fifth grade, she
began replacing them with a new group of friends. Suddenly
Tabi's parents began to notice that their daughter was becoming overly concerned about losing weight. She refused to eat
certain foods that she thought were fattening.

Her parents then received a call from the school nurse, who
said that Tabi had begun skipping lunch at school. She had
called Tabi to her office and weighed her, and her weight
had dropped since her summer physical.

Thinking that her concern about her weight only reflected
her unhappiness about losing her old friends, her parents decided not to make a big fuss about Tabi's dieting. They also
decided to have a talk with her that evening. "Tabi, we're
concerned about your eating habits," her father said. "We
know that you are interested in having a healthy diet, but
skipping lunch is not the way to keep healthy."

"But I'm getting so fat!" Tabi moaned. "None of my old
friends like me because I've gotten so fat!"

"Did someone say that you were fat?" her father asked.

"Yes, Billy Michaels called me 'fatso' on the playground when I missed a fly ball during a kickball game," Tabi replied.

"So because your friends aren't playing with you anymore and a boy calls you fat, that makes it true?" her father questioned.

"Well, it is true!" Tabi answered defiantly.

"But the school nurse said you had actually lost weight since summer. That's not a healthy direction for weight to go in while you're still growing," her mother noted.

"The nurse is lying! I'm getting fat and I know it!" Tabi shrieked despondently.

"Why would your nurse want to lie? What would she have to gain by that?" Tabi's mother asked, keeping a calm but sincere tone to her voice.

Tabi couldn't answer that question. Her concern about her weight was being shaken.

During the next week, no one said anything negative about Tabi's eating habits. However, her parents did tell her that they were glad she was taking good care of herself when they saw she was eating sensibly.

Tabi's new friends began to appear at her house from time to time, and Tabi seemed somewhat happier. She and her mother began to plan meals together, and the nurse reported that Tabi was eating her lunch.

Tabi's parents knew that not making a fuss or demanding that she eat had been the best route to take toward helping Tabi cope with her problem. However, they also resolved to take her to a counselor if the problem came up again, being aware that a youngster's obsessions with diets can be a life-threatening symptom of underlying problems.

Sleeplessness

("I'm too worried to go to sleep!")

∿∿∿∿∿∿∿∿∿∿∿∿∿∿∿∿∿∿∿∿∿∿∿∿∿∿∿∿∿∿∿∿∿

"Our house creaks! Our floors groan!" your child shrieks when she calls you from her room complaining that your house is haunted. But listen closely. When your child moans that she cannot go to sleep, she is really saying that she wants to get some thoughts off her chest or some more fun under her belt.

Allow her to tell you what's on her mind when she says that she can't sleep. But do not allow her to manipulate the staying-in-bed rule. Set some time aside in the going-to-bed routine (not *after* her lights-out time) to talk about the events of the day in a no-hurry, no-worry mood. Your child will then go to slumberland with a clearer mind.

PREVENTING THE PROBLEM

PROBLEM-SOLVE AT BEDTIME. Set up time to talk about the events of the day as part of the going-to-bed routine so that your child can clear her mind of troubling situations. Helping her arrive at solutions to daily problems increases the chances that she will be able to relax enough to go to sleep peacefully.

MODEL A WORRY-FREE APPROACH TO LIFE. Avoid worrying about life's problems by using a logical problem-solving model to manage life's routine ups and downs. (See PROBLEM-SOLVING in the "Discipline Dictionary.")

KEEP A CONSISTENT BEDTIME. Children who go to bed according to a specific routine and at a consistent time have fewer going-to-sleep problems.

SOLVING THE PROBLEM

What to Do

HELP YOUR CHILD RELAX AT BEDTIME.
Teach your child how to relax at bedtime to help her go to sleep more easily. Say relaxing words, such as "smooth, calm, quiet, and soft," and encourage her to use them over and over again in order to establish a sense of calm within her.

ALLOW READING AT BEDTIME.
A child who can't go to sleep easily may be able to relax by reading a nonviolent, soothing book, because doing so will turn her thoughts away from her own concerns.

GIVE YOUR CHILD PERMISSION TO BE AWAKE.
A child often worries that her parents will be upset if she can't sleep. Telling your child that not being able to sleep is "no big deal" will put her mind at ease.

GIVE YOUR CHILD THE FACTS ABOUT SLEEPLESSNESS.
If she is unable to go to sleep, your child may worry about not being able to do her work well in school the next day. Tell her that her being unable to go to sleep will not damage her achievement though it may make her cranky.

What Not to Do

DON'T MAKE BEDTIME AND SLEEP OVERLY IMPORTANT.
Exaggerating the importance of sleep will only encourage a child to worry about not being able to fall asleep easily.

AVOID PRE-BEDTIME HASSLES. A child may
have difficulty going to sleep if she is worried that her parents
are fighting or are angry with her.

AVOID THE HOMEWORK TRAP. Help your child
keep track of her homework assignments and encourage her to
complete homework immediately after school or early in the
evening. This will prevent her late-night worrying about her
performance at school the next day.

DON'T PUT OFF PROBLEM-SOLVING. It is
better to problem-solve with your child before she goes to bed
than to take the chance that a problem will cause her so much
concern that she won't be able to go to sleep.

~~~~~~~~~~~~~~~~~~~~~~~~~~~~~~~~~~~~~

Getting It Off Angie's Chest

"I can't sleep!" was eleven-year-old Angie Struck's nightly
bedtime song. On one particular night, Mrs. Struck finally
got angry and Angie began crying, which further prevented
her from going to sleep.

Angie's mom decided to try a new going-to-bed routine.
She wasn't sure if it would quiet Angie's favorite refrain, but
she wanted to try.

"Angie, let's talk about your day," Mrs. Struck began on
the first night of the plan. "How did school go?"

As Angie began to relate the events of the day, she involved
her mother in helping her cope with her disappointment over
a test or in problem-solving her fights with friends.

"So Jennifer has decided not to speak to you for a while,"
her mother reflected. "What do you think you could do about
that?"

"I hate it when she gets like that! But I think I could ignore
her," Angie suggested.

"Is there anything else that you can think of that you could do?" her mother continued.

"Well, I could talk to her about why she is mad at me," she offered.

"What do you think would happen if you did that?" Mrs. Struck asked patiently, letting Angie take the lead in the conversation.

"Maybe we could figure out some way to be friends again," Angie answered brightly.

"Do you want to pretend I'm Jennifer and try it now?" her mother asked.

They role-played for a few minutes until Angie felt comfortable with how she was going to approach her friend and what she would say.

Angie continued to calm down even more by doing the following relaxation exercise that her mother taught her: She thought about her feet feeling heavy; then she imagined her ankles, knees, thighs, and stomach also feeling heavy until she was relaxed all over.

Her mother kissed her and said, "Good night, sweetheart. I love you. Remember, if you don't go to sleep in a few minutes, just read until you are tired enough to sleep."

Angie nodded, closed her eyes, and soon was fast asleep. Going to sleep wasn't always as easy for Angie as it was on that first night, but she soon discovered that not going to sleep quickly and easily was no big deal when she didn't upset herself over it.

Poor Personal Hygiene

("I hate showers!")

∿∿∿∿∿∿∿∿∿∿∿∿∿∿∿∿∿∿∿∿∿∿∿∿∿∿∿∿

What constitutes getting clean in your mind may be miles of soapsuds away from what it means to your childolescent. Before fighting daily battles over whether or not to shampoo, it is important for you to separate your child from his dirt. It's not him who "stinks," it's his sweat, grime, and grass stains. The issue then becomes you and him against the dirt, not the dirt and him against you. Teach your child the ABC's of good grooming, though he may not appreciate the whys. What he will appreciate, is that choosing to get clean is the ticket to doing what he wants to do, such as playing with friends the next day.

PREVENTING THE PROBLEM

MAKE WASHING AND BATHING A PART OF A DAILY ROUTINE. A child needs routine in order to remember what he is required to do. When you allow your child to skip bathing for several days, he may get confused about when he needs to clean up, and will be more likely to protest when he finally has to do so.

USE A CHECKLIST AS A REMINDER. Checklists offer structure and serve as nag-free reminders. Create a checklist for your child to follow, including those grooming goals you would like to see met each day and those which can be accomplished less frequently.

PRAISE YOUR CHILD FOR GOOD GROOMING.

The best encouragement your child can have is your praise. Say, "You must have worked hard to get your hands clean. Aren't you proud of yourself?" Praise his meeting the grooming goals established on the checklist, as well as the effort made to do so.

MODEL GROOMING SKILLS.

Show your child how to maintain a clean, well-groomed appearance by allowing him to watch you as you get ready for the day. When your child sees you well-groomed, he learns what social expectations exist in the world.

SEPARATE YOUR CHILD FROM HIS DIRT.

Say, "I love you, but I don't like how your hair smells," to communicate the message that you always accept your child, if not always his behavior.

SOLVING THE PROBLEM

What to Do

BE FIRM ABOUT GROOMING GOALS.

Your child needs to know that some requirements are nonnegotiable. For example, if your child's good-grooming rule is to bathe every day, that rule is not changed by his whining, begging, or playing "let's make a deal." Counter your child's attempts to change his routine by saying, "Yes, I understand that you don't want to take a bath, but you know the rule. When you have finished bathing, then you may watch your favorite program on television."

CHECK YOUR CHILD FOR COMPLIANCE.

When your child is required to bathe, shampoo, or simply to wash his hands for dinner, check closely for his compliance.

Keep in mind that your child's having wet hair doesn't necessarily mean that he has taken a shower. If you catch your child trying to fake a shower, motivate him to follow your rules in the future by enforcing these consequences: He must return to the shower while you supervise his clean-up routine and he loses a privilege for the remainder of the day. Say, "I'm sorry that you chose not to take your shower; that means you've also chosen not to play chess tonight."

MAKE BATHING A FUN EXPERIENCE. Provide your child with his own easy-to-use products, and appropriate stylish tools of the trade (bubble bath, soap, combs, and so on).

MAKE SURE BATHING PRODUCTS ARE WITHIN YOUR CHILD'S REACH. Don't leave your child high and dry without access to his bathing products.

What Not to Do

DON'T NAG YOUR CHILD ABOUT GROOMING. Nagging only encourages your child to be dependent on parental reminders. Moreover, children don't like to be nagged by their parents, and are more likely to be rebellious when they are nagged.

DON'T IMPOSE PUNISHMENT FOR NON-COMPLIANCE. Harsh punishment for failure to meet good grooming goals will only make your child angry and vindictive. Instead, use natural consequences for noncompliance and praise for compliance with good-grooming rules. Say, "I'm sorry you chose not to shampoo. I want you to know how to wash your hair when you need to. Let's practice." Then go back to the shower together and supervise the process.

∿∿∿∿∿∿∿∿∿∿∿∿∿∿∿∿∿∿∿∿∿∿∿

Grimy Greg

Greg never seemed to get soap and water past his hands. "You need a shower," Mrs. Majors would say to her eight-year-old son whenever her nose caught wind of him.

"Okay. I'll take one before I go to bed tonight," Greg would answer amiably. But after Greg came downstairs from having taken his shower, his hair wet and his pajamas on, his mother always noticed that his odor had not changed.

"You don't smell any better than when you went up to shower!" she'd exclaim. "Are you sure you washed?"

"Sure did," Greg would answer quickly as he left the room.

Realizing that their son seemed not to know how to bathe himself correctly, Greg's parents formulated a hygiene plan and presented it to him one night.

"Greg, we know you have a thousand things you would rather do than shower, bathe, or shampoo, but being clean is important," Mr. Majors began. "So we have come up with an easy plan to help you stay clean. Here's how it will work: Each evening before bed, you will take a shower and shampoo your hair. After your shower, we will inspect you, and you will earn points for being clean. You can cash the points in for extra privileges like staying up later at night or having extra television-watching time. If you aren't clean, then you will have to go back and wash until you are clean. Do you understand the deal?" his dad concluded.

"I think so," Greg responded, brushing off the instruction-session lightly.

That night after his shower, he presented himself to his parents. His hair was wet, but it didn't smell like shampoo. His dad lifted his pajama top and lightly touched the boy's stomach, noting how sticky his skin was.

"It looks like we have to supervise your shower more

closely," Mr. Majors said as he led his son back to the bath-room.

This time Greg scrubbed himself and was squeaky clean when he emerged from the shower. His parents praised his cleanliness. The next night, they supervised him again, but the following night, they just conducted the inspection. Greg was clean, so he was granted the privilege of staying up an extra fifteen minutes. He enjoyed the additional time as he snuggled his clean body between his parents and watched television with them.

Gradually cleanliness, which had been a chore before, be-came an important part of Greg's daily routine.

Self-Image
Problems

∿∿∿∿∿∿∿∿∿∿∿∿∿∿∿∿∿∿∿∿∿∿∿∿∿∿∿∿∿∿∿∿∿∿

Being Excessively Competitive

("We should have won! The other team didn't play fair!")

∧∧∧∧∧∧∧∧∧∧∧∧∧∧∧∧∧∧∧∧∧∧∧∧∧∧∧∧∧∧∧∧∧∧

If your child focuses more on the need to win than on the desire to learn the game and play for fun, think about where your own priorities are placed. Do you value winning over playing the game? Then, help your child learn to cope with the competitive game of life—a game that inevitably has some losers and some winners. When your child discovers that she is less talented than others in a certain sport or academic subject, help her swallow this hard dose of real-life medicine by telling her that what she does and who she is are two separate things. She may lose in a competitive situation, but she is not a loser!

PREVENTING THE PROBLEM

DON'T START CHILDREN IN SPORTS TOO SOON. Start your child in the competitive game-playing scene when she is mature enough to handle the pressure of trying to live up to her coaches' and your demands.

GO WITH YOUR CHILD TO SPORTS OR ACADEMIC COMPETITIONS. Support your child in her sports activities. She will be more likely to stick with a sport, learn its rules, and understand the methods of play better than a child whose parents stay home during game

time. In addition, if you go to the games, you will be able to see whether coaches and parents are modeling good sportsmanship. If they are not, discuss with them ways to correct their bad examples. If your efforts fail and you believe that the adults' behavior is truly harmful, consider removing your child from the team.

MODEL GOOD SPORTSMANSHIP. If you demonstrate good sportsmanship as you participate in your child's sports competitions, then she will be more likely to become a good sport. Being involved in sportsmanship councils, giving sportsmanship awards, and insisting on good sportsmanship from parents and coaches provide a good model for your child.

SOLVING THE PROBLEM

What to Do

OFFER CONSEQUENCES FOR GOOD AND BAD SPORTSMANSHIP. Reward your child with praise for demonstrating good sportsmanship. Say, "You acted like such a good sport when you helped that other player up after she was knocked down." If your child behaves like a poor sport, say, "I'm sorry you refused to shake hands with that other player. That wasn't good sportsmanship. When you show good sportsmanship during the next game, I will allow you to have your friend over this week." This message tells your child what behavior you expect and lets her know that you will enforce Grandma's Rule if the good sportsmanship rule is broken. (See GRANDMA'S RULE in the "Discipline Dictionary.")

ALLOW YOUR CHILD TO VENT HER FRUSTRATION. After you let your child express her anger at a game loss, use the situation as a launching pad for a discussion about sportsmanship. Focus on what could have been done to try to win the last game, so that the issue is no longer simply losing or winning but rather learning what skills were exhibited and what improvement is needed in those skills.

INTERVENE WHEN YOU SEE POOR SPORTSMANSHIP BEING MODELED. If you see coaches or parents displaying poor sportsmanship, don't hesitate to make suggestions. Often parent groups, athletic associations, school administrations, and others are interested in fostering good sportsmanship and are willing to work with coaches and parents to change the attitudes of teams that become overly competitive. Instead of criticizing the violators, suggest ways to avoid those problems in the future.

What Not to Do

DON'T ASK ABOUT THE OUTCOME OF THE COMPETITION. Asking your child if she won or lost sets up winning as more important than it is. Talk instead about the game, the skills needed, and the improvement desired to develop those skills.

DON'T BE A POOR SPORT. When you become overly upset about the outcome of a game or about the coaching or officiating, your child sees you as a role model of sportsmanship—but an inappropriate one. Even if you disagree with the outcome of a game, support your child in her performance and talk about future games and game strategies.

DON'T BE CRITICAL OF YOUR CHILD'S PLAY. Contrary to popular belief, there is no such thing as constructive criticism. Criticism only tears down; it doesn't build. Criticism only tells what wasn't done, not what can be done. If your child made errors in play, accept that as part of human nature and the nature of sports. Then suggest ways to correct the errors. At no time does the error have to be pointed out. Instead, say, "May I help you with your defense? I may be able to show you how you can prevent that player from getting by you." This focuses on correcting the problem, not on the problem itself.

DON'T CRITICIZE THE COACHES. Although you may disagree with the coaching strategies, don't make critical comments about the coach to your child. This challenges her loyalty to her coach and her team. Again, support her playing and discuss her game plan.

Where Has All the Fun Gone?

Justin Gordon lived and died for baseball. When he was eight, he joined a baseball team on which he played his heart out for the next two years.

Unfortunately, during the games, he learned more than just how to play ball: He was exposed to the verbal abuse of parents and coaches. If the parents om the bleachers didn't like the way the umpires called the games, rude and crude taunts would pour out of the stands. Even the players got into the act by riding the umpires from the dugout and yelling insults at the other teams. When they lost, the boys would often refuse to shake hands with the winning teams.

One day, Justin was thrown out of a game because he yelled at the umpire about a call. His parents were upset with the umpire for a while, but then realized that Justin and his team had been acting very unsportsmanlike for some time now.

They called the coach for a meeting and, together with some of the other interested parents, they made up a set of sportsmanship rules. First, parents were requested to refrain from shouting insults from the stands. Second, the boys were instructed to shake the hands of the opposing team after each game. Third, the boys were asked to stay in the dugout any time they weren't at bat or on the field and to refrain from shouting anything but encouragement. Any taunts, insults, or arguments with the umpire would result in automatic benching. The boys and their parents were asked to sign the agreement.

In addition, Justin's parents commented after each game on specific instances of good sportsmanship, although these were difficult to find at first. "Justin, although you boys lost the game today, you played well and you were good sports about the outcome," his father commented one day after a particularly well-played game. "You must be proud of yourselves for being such good sports."

"Yeah, but we didn't win," Justin sulked.

"I know you like to win, but somebody has to lose in each game," his father countered matter-of-factly. "If you can't stand to lose, maybe you shouldn't play. What do you suppose the big league players do when they lose a game?"

"I guess they think about the next game," Justin suggested.

"I'll bet they also think about the mistakes they made and how to correct them. If they never lost or made mistakes, they wouldn't learn new things to do to make themselves better."

Being better at baseball was a meaningful goal for Justin, so he began to learn from his mistakes how to play better ball, not how to get angry at his opponent.

Wanting to Be Perfect

("I can't believe I missed that word on my spelling test! What a jerk I am.")

∿∿∿∿∿∿∿∿∿∿∿∿∿∿∿∿∿∿∿∿∿∿∿

Perfectionism is a natural part of some children's personalities, and it is better for you to accept your perfectionist child than try to change him. You can, however, teach him that being perfect is an unattainable goal. Because he always views himself as not quite good enough, he needs to be taught how to accept the gray area of life—where most people, places, and things do fall.

PREVENTING THE PROBLEM

MODEL ACCEPTANCE OF MISTAKES. If you can accept mistakes in yourself, you will create an atmosphere of acceptance for your child. When you don't spell a word right on a thank-you note, for example, say, "Oh, well, I've made a mistake. It's no big deal; I can handle it." This kind of statement tells your child that adults can make mistakes and accept themselves as mistake-makers, so it must be okay for children to make mistakes, too. Then calmly correct your error so that your child can see how to correct a mistake patiently, as well.

GIVE UNCONDITIONAL LOVE TO YOUR CHILD. A child needs parental love, and that love needs to be given without conditions. "I think you can do better," is a conditional statement. If you say this when your child makes a mistake on a spelling test, your child gets the message that he is not quite good enough and must change.

Rather than point out his errors, it is more helpful to say to him, "You did a very nice job on these words. Now, let's see if you can spell the other words correctly, too."

SOLVING THE PROBLEM

What to Do

PLAY THE GOOD DAY GAME. To avoid your child's developing a critical view of the world, ask him to tell you five good things about a person he's criticizing or about his day.

HELP YOUR CHILD USE HIS OWN LOGIC TO SEE THAT PERFECTIONISM IS AN UNREACHABLE GOAL. When his complaints start becoming habitual, ask, "How does getting a C on a test make you stupid?" If your child cannot answer that question or tells you that it makes him stupid because he didn't know the answer, then you need to explain to him the difference between intelligence and knowledge.

MAKE PERFECTIONISM MORE EXPENSIVE. If your child always complains about being imperfect, raise the cost of these complaints by assigning him a job for each one. Say, "I'm sorry you've chosen to continue to call yourself stupid. You will now have to work for me to make up for putting yourself down like that."

PRAISE BEHAVIOR THAT IS NOT PERFECTIONIST. In the absence of your child's complaints about not being perfect, praise his ability to cope with imperfection. Say, "It is really good that you didn't call yourself stupid when you made those mistakes on your math paper. It must feel good to be so accepting of yourself."

ACCEPT YOUR CHILD FOR WHO HE IS. Often parents judge their child by what he produces rather than by who he is. Accepting your child for who he is simply means putting your arm around his shoulder and giving him a hug, even though his behavior has not been acceptable.

TEACH PROBLEM-SOLVING. Children who become upset when they make errors often don't know how to go about solving the problems that caused the errors. If this is the case with your child, brainstorm solutions to the problem with him. When a list of solutions has been made, evaluate each solution's potential outcome and then choose one that can be successfully applied to the problem at hand.

What Not to Do

DON'T OVERREACT TO ERRORS. If your child drops a plate of cookies you made, don't say, "Why did you do that? Don't you know better?" Instead of getting angry, say, "I'm sorry you dropped the cookies. I know it was an accident and accidents happen—none of us is perfect."

AVOID THE PERFECTIONISM TRAP. Sometimes a child learns that he can get your attention by becoming overly upset by his errors. Avoid this trap by keeping your cool and guiding your child into acceptance rather than giving him sympathy for having made a mistake.

〜〜〜〜〜〜〜〜〜〜〜〜〜〜〜〜〜〜

Mistake-Proof Paul

Paul Katz was a firstborn child whose parents had always expected him to do well in anything he tried. They began to realize how much pressure they must be putting on their son when his perfectionism began to take over his second-grade school life. His parents vowed to do something about their demands and their reactions to Paul's errors.

Paul's mother had always believed that somehow her son wouldn't do well unless he was reminded. But the next morning as Paul left for school, she fought the old urge to say, "Do your best!" and substituted, "I love you, Paul!" as he bounded out the door.

When he came home that evening with a backpack full of books and papers, Paul and his parents sat down to go over his schoolwork. He tried to hide papers with errors or grades that were below 100 percent.

"Oh, Paul, you really did a nice job on this paper. Look how many you got right," his mother commented about one of the papers that he was trying to stash under his seat.

"But I didn't get everything right!" Paul lamented.

"That's okay, Paul. Nobody gets everything right all the time. We all make mistakes. Now let's look at what you got right on some of the other papers."

After several weeks of support and encouragement, Paul began to accept imperfections in his work. His mother would ask him to correct his mistakes, so he wouldn't think sloppy work was okay; and she stopped making any criticisms of Paul.

Both his parents also stopped trying to demand perfection from themselves, understanding that it would be difficult for Paul to accept himself—mistakes and all—if they did not model this behavior for him.

Feeling Overly Fearful

("I can't go in there. It's too scary!")

〰〰〰〰〰〰〰〰〰〰〰〰〰〰〰

"Mom! Come quick! There's a bug!" your six-year-old yells at the sight of an ant. When a child displays unreasonable fear, she is saying that she doesn't know how to cope with certain experiences. Use this opportunity to help her learn that her feelings are valid and that you care enough about her to believe what she says. After establishing that basic sense of trust, focus on helping your child cope with her fears. Ask her what it is about bugs that makes her afraid. Brainstorm ways that she can choose to make herself unafraid. Teach her that she alone has the power to make herself afraid or unafraid of anything in life.

Note: Phobic children generally have a long history of fears and phobias, and often there is a family history of similar problems, including depression. If, after trying some of the suggestions you find here, your child is still having phobic problems, seek professional help.

PREVENTING THE PROBLEM

HELP YOUR CHILD LEARN TO COPE WITH FEAR.
If you teach your child how to cope with her fears rather than trying to take the fears away, she will have a better chance of overcoming her fears in the future. Say, "Yes, I understand that you are afraid of grasshoppers. But you're brave and strong, and you can handle being near them. I

know you can!" This allows your child to use her own strength to overcome fear.

MODEL COPING WITH FEARS. When you feel afraid, talk about your fear with your child and show her how you are working to overcome it. For instance, remind yourself of the facts about a scary situation. Say to your child, "I'm afraid of flying in airplanes. But I know that the airplanes I fly in are checked for problems before they are allowed to take off. So I will just be brave and trust the mechanics and pilots to do their jobs correctly. I know I can handle this."

SOLVING THE PROBLEM

What to Do

TEACH COPING WITH FEAR IN SMALL DOSES. If your child says, "I'm scared to go to bed in the dark," believe her. Instead of saying, "That's silly. You're not really afraid. There's nothing to be afraid of," say, "I understand that you are afraid. But you are brave and strong and can handle being in a dark room."

PRAISE COPING WITH FEARS. As your child confronts her fears, praise her coping with them. Say to your child who is afraid of school, "You are being so brave. I understand that you don't want to go to school, but you are handling going very well. I'll bet you will do even better tomorrow."

OFFER REWARDS FOR COPING. Ways to extinguish fears include giving privileges as rewards rather than presents (material objects). Material objects are things that a child has and doesn't have to do anything to keep. Privileges get used up and must be won again by doing the desired behavior.

Initially, a reward might be: "For spending the night in your own bed each night this week, I will take you to lunch on Saturday," or "Because you went to school today without getting upset, I will meet you after school at the park."

USE GRANDMA'S RULE. By telling your child ahead of time about the privileges to be granted for coping with a fear, you will be giving her an incentive to work toward the goal of not acting fearfully. Say, "When you can go to school without crying, then we can go to the skateboard shop after school to look for the new ramp you have been saving for."

What Not to Do

DON'T SUBSTITUTE SYMPATHY FOR EMPATHY. By saying things such as, "I understand how you feel" and "I've felt that way before," your empathy communicates your understanding of your child and her problem with the fear. Your sympathy, on the other hand, gives your child the message that it is okay for her to hold on to her fear because you will eliminate the fearful situation. She has no way of learning how to cope with her fears. Taking a child into bed with you at night when she is afraid of the dark, for example, only encourages her to avoid what she fears; allowing her to miss school when she is afraid to go doesn't let her learn to face the unknown challenges of the world.

DON'T TRY TO PUNISH AWAY FEARS. Threatening your child if she doesn't get over her fear doesn't teach her how to cope with her fear, either, it only teaches her to fear more things. Saying, "If you don't get back in your bed, I'm going to spank you," or "If you don't go to school, the truant officer will put you in jail," only substitutes another fear for the one your child already has.

DON'T BELITTLE YOUR CHILD. Saying, "Don't be such a baby! Big girls go to school!" only tells your child that she is unable to cope. It doesn't give her the affirmation she needs to develop coping skills. When children are belittled, they end up feeling even less capable of handling their fears.

〰〰〰〰〰〰〰〰〰〰〰〰〰〰〰〰〰〰〰

Fearing the Worst

As a preschooler, Charlie Cashion was always hesitant to do things. His mother, Mrs. Cashion, was very cautious with him, often reminding him to watch out or be careful.

By the time he turned seven, he did seem to be afraid of everything. He couldn't stay in his bed at night because he heard the creaks and groans of the house, and the noises frightened him. He wouldn't spend the night at a friend's because he was afraid. His buddies began to tease him about being "chicken," which only made him more afraid.

Charlie was having a problem coping with so many things that his parents decided to teach him how to recognize what was dangerous and what wasn't, and to offer him rewards for learning to cope with his fears. They started with helping him overcome his fears at bedtime.

"Charlie, we understand that you are afraid when you go to bed and that there are lots of strange noises that occur in the night," his dad began.

"Yeah, Dad! And I think it's somebody trying to break in," Charlie blurted. "I'm afraid they'll come into my room and kill me."

"Charlie, when was the last time that somebody broke into our house?" his dad countered.

"Well . . . never, I guess," Charlie admitted.

"When was the last time somebody broke into a house in the neighborhood?"

"I don't think ever," Charlie answered slowly.

"What are the chances that somebody would pick this house and then pick your room to come in to murder you?" Mr. Cashion wanted to know.

"Not very likely, I guess," Charlie offered.

"That's right. Now, I'll tell you what," his dad proposed. "If you can stay in your bed tonight, then you can sleep on the floor in our room in your sleeping bag tomorrow night." That was one of Charlie's favorite things to do.

When Charlie went to bed that night, his parents reminded him that he was brave and strong and could handle the fear he had of the house. And handle it he did. The next day, he claimed not to have slept all night. But he did stay in his bed, so he was rewarded the privilege of sleeping on the floor of his parents' room.

Then his parents made this new contract: For staying in his bed for two nights, he could earn one night of being able to sleep in his parents' room. Gradually, the number of nights that he slept in his room grew and grew. Other fears of Charlie's also began to fall away as he gained more confidence. His parents and he set new contracts for other fears, and slowly he was learning how to cope with the objects of his fears, even though he didn't *like* them.

Boasting and Bragging

("I'm the best pitcher on the baseball team!")

∧∧∧∧∧∧∧∧∧∧∧∧∨∨∨∨∨∨∨∨∨∨∨∨∧∧∧

Because a childolescent bases his self-concept on the approval or disapproval of his peers, he believes that he must always find ways to impress and amaze his friends—a tough act to keep up every day, every hour of the day. Central to the process of helping your child understand that he does not need to boast and brag is telling him that you love him unconditionally—no matter what he says or does. His self-acceptance will be strengthened when you repeat this love song, while you focus on his *behavior* rather than on *him*.

Note: It is important to know the difference between simple factual statements of pride ("My dad is the best dad in the world!") and boasting to make oneself look better ("My dad is better than your dad!"). To differentiate pride from braggadocio, consider your child's intent in stating his feelings. Ask yourself: Was he trying to impress someone or was he expressing his feelings?

PREVENTING THE PROBLEM

MODEL WAYS OF TAKING PRIDE IN AC-COMPLISHMENTS.
When you show your child how you can take pride in your accomplishments without bragging about what you have done, you set the stage for your child to talk about what he has done without bragging. Say, "My boss was really pleased with the job I did on that project. I

really felt good that I was able to do well." Reinforce similar statements when your child makes them. If he says, "I got a hundred percent on my spelling paper!" you can respond with, "You must be proud of yourself for working so hard and earning that good grade."

SOLVING THE PROBLEM

What to Do

SET GUIDELINES. Your child may not recognize that bragging is inappropriate behavior. To help him understand the nature of bragging, teach him a new way of making a statement that sounded like bragging. His saying, "I can pitch better than anybody," can be restated into saying, "My coach thinks I am a good pitcher. I have good control and don't walk many batters." Show your child how the restatement allows him to express pride in his accomplishment, tells where the information came from, and gives evidence that supports his statement.

HELP YOUR CHILD FEEL GOOD ABOUT HIS ACCOMPLISHMENTS. Children often believe that they must perform well to be loved and accepted. You can help your child overcome this self-destructive belief by helping him focus on his own good feelings about what he has accomplished. Saying, "You must have really felt good when you hit that home run," or "You must be so proud of all of the effort that you put into that math paper," helps your child become less dependent on the approval of others and more self-approving.

What Not to Do

DON'T BRAG AND BOAST. Often parents want to show off their own accomplishments; however, if they do so, they are only modeling bragging for their child. Make sure you state your accomplishments in a factual way without boasting.

DON'T IDENTIFY YOUR CHILD WITH HIS BEHAVIOR. Keep your child and his behavior firmly separated and show that separation in the way you talk. For example, avoid the use of "good boy" and "good girl" in praise. Simply point out what your child has done that was appropriate or inappropriate.

DON'T OVERREACT TO YOUR CHILD'S BRAGGING. Getting upset over your child's bragging reinforces the problem. For example, if you punish your child by shouting or grounding him for boasting, you only create feelings of inadequacy in him that may cause him to think that he really *does* need to boast and brag in order to be loved.

∿∿∿∿∿∿∿∿∿∿∿∿∿∿∿∿∿∿∿∿∿∿∿∿

Big-Shot Billy

Twelve-year-old Billy McCorkle was always bragging about what a great athlete he was; but instead of bringing him more friends, his behavior only isolated him more. Nobody wanted to be around him because he always wanted to be the center of attention.

"We need to do something about Billy's bragging," Mr. McCorkle said one evening. "I was talking to his baseball coach today, and he said that all of the kids were complaining to him about Billy."

"His teacher told me the same thing," Billy's mother answered. "It's gotten to be quite a problem."

The next day, Billy's mom met with his teacher to try to get some help and found her willing and ready to talk. "Billy seems to have a poor self-concept," Mrs. North, his teacher began. "It probably started last year when he got behind in reading and had to go to the special reading teacher for a while. Being singled out for special help seemed to make him feel inferior to his classmates," she continued.

That night Billy's mom shared this information with her husband. "We were really hard on Billy last year when he was struggling with reading, and his teacher thinks it affected his self-concept," she reported.

"And think about how many times I criticized him for making mistakes in baseball. I'm sure he believes he has to be perfect for us to love him," his dad offered.

They decided on a plan to praise Billy for his accomplishments with no mention of his errors. If he made mistakes, they would give him a hug and help him improve if he wanted. They would also help him find new ways of telling of his accomplishments without bragging about them.

"I'm the best pitcher on the team!" he bragged to his teammate, Sam, after the game that Saturday. After Sam went home, his mother said, "Billy, when you told Sam that you were the best pitcher today, I wondered if you could have told him about your pitching so that it didn't sound like bragging."

"I guess I could just have told him my strikeout record, or I could have thought of something else to talk about," he answered slowly.

"That's right. You aren't a better person because you are a good pitcher. That's just a talent you were given," his mother suggested.

As Billy's parents praised him for his good work and accepted him for who he was (not for what he did), he began to be happier and more content with himself, apart from his accomplishments.

Overemphasizing Clothing

("It's my body and I can put anything I want on it!")

∧∧∧∧∧∧∧∧∧∧∧∧∧∧∧∧∧∧∧∧∧∧∧∧∧∧∧∧∧∧∧∧∧∧∧∧

You know what your child *should* wear and she knows what she *wants* to wear. These closet clashes are fueled by the fact that children are constantly being bombarded—mostly through television—with the latest fashion ideas just at the stage in their development when they are beginning to evaluate their own wardrobes by what their peers are wearing. Set down rules for what is appropriate attire for different occasions and establish rewards for following these rules when making buying and wearing decisions. By doing so, your child will be learning what she needs to know about clothing protocol; and you will avoid becoming the "fashion enemy" by letting the impartial rule be the control.

PREVENTING THE PROBLEM

HELP YOUR CHILD DEVELOP A GOOD SELF-CONCEPT. A child can learn to feel good about herself by making connections with her family, friends, and school; by her being allowed to have some control over her life; and by setting goals for herself. A child who feels good about herself is less likely to think about her own worth in terms of her clothing.

DISCOURAGE JUDGING PEOPLE BY THEIR CLOTHING. You can set the family tone by reducing your

own emphasis on the importance of clothing in judging people. If your child is taught to focus on someone's personal characteristics rather than on her material possessions, she will be less likely to dress for others.

IF YOU DON'T WANT YOUR CHILD TO WEAR SOMETHING, DON'T BUY IT OR LET HER BUY IT.

BUY CLOTHING WITH YOUR CHILD TO EN-SURE THAT YOU ARE IN AGREEMENT WITH HER CHOICES.

SOLVING THE PROBLEM

What to Do

SET LIMITS TO CLOTHING SELECTION. A child needs to learn to select her own clothing, but she also needs to follow certain rules when making clothing choices. If she wants to wear clothing that is inappropriate for the weather, let the outside temperature be the rule. Say, "You may wear shorts if the morning temperature is above seventy degrees." Set other rules about what clothing may be worn to different activities (church, ice skating, and so on); if she picks inappropriate clothes, remind her of the rule by saying, "What's the rule about what we wear for church?"

ALLOW YOUR CHILD TO MAKE CLOTHING CHOICES THE NIGHT BEFORE SCHOOL.

When your child lays out her clothes the night before school, she will avoid clothing-selection dilemmas in the morning.

SET LIMITS TO PAYING THE PRICE OF DESIGNER CLOTHING. When a child tries to coerce you into buying expensive designer labels, remember who is paying for them. You may choose to say No to a particular purchase or set a limited price on what you will pay for it and allow your child to match that amount. Say, "I will give you the amount needed for this brand of jeans, but if you want the designer label, you can pay the difference with your money."

FOLLOW YOUR RULES. If you believe that it is inappropriate to spend extra money for expensive clothing, say to your child, "No, I don't believe that anyone in this family needs to wear designer labels." Discuss your values with your child so that she will understand why you believe as you do.

What Not to Do

DON'T EXPECT TO LIKE ALL CHOICES YOUR CHILD MAKES IN WHAT SHE WEARS. Instead, let her select from appropriate choices.

DON'T GET INTO ARGUMENTS ABOUT CLOTHING. Instead of falling into the trap of arguing about clothing, simply say, "What's the rule about that choice of clothing?" This teaches your child that there are rules to be followed when making decisions about dressing for a certain occasion.

DON'T OVEREMPHASIZE CLOTHING. Modeling good taste in clothing selections without focusing all your attention on it allows your child to see that adults can be casual about clothing.

Back to Basics

Every morning, ten-year-old Brooke Belzer and her mother fought over what Brooke would wear to school. She wanted to wear what was "cool," but her mother wanted her to wear what she thought looked nice.

"I'll die if I have to wear that!" Brooke would wail about her mother's clothing selection. "Everybody will make fun of me in that."

"No they won't, and stop making such a fuss!" Mrs. Belzer would counter, but Brooke was not to be appeased.

Eventually, Brooke's choices would prevail, because in order to keep her from being late for school, her mother would let her wear anything she wanted. And so the clothing wars continued.

Finally tiring of the battles, Mrs. Belzer formulated a new plan one night. When Brooke came home from school the next day, her mother launched into her game plan with her.

"Brooke, I've decided that because we can't seem to agree on what you will wear to school every morning, we should do things differently. Let's go to your room and go through your clothes to pick out what will be school clothes and what will be play clothes. Then, each night, we can lay out what you will wear to school the next day."

They disagreed over the play versus school placement of some items; and in those instances, Brooke's mother let her daughter make another kind of decision. "If we can't agree, then the item goes to charity," she explained. "You decide. Do you want to keep this red blouse or give it to charity?"

Brooke decided to keep the blouse and several other items and put them in the play pile rather than the school pile, as her mother suggested. Every night, when they would pick out an outfit for the next day, Brooke wanted to bring clothing out of the play group; but her mother blocked the move each time.

"Remember, it was decided that those would be play clothes. If they continue to cause trouble, they will have to go to charity," she would comment.

When one outfit was given to charity because it was "causing trouble," Brooke realized that her mother was firm in her decision. After a while, Brooke began to understand that no matter what she wore, her friends liked her. Even if some made fun of her because she dressed according to her house rules, she decided that it was better to learn about what clothing was and was not appropriate so that she could make wise choices on her own, rather than always do what her friends wanted.

Activities

Boredom

("Mom, what can I do? There's nothing to do around here—I'm bored!")

〜〜〜〜〜〜〜〜〜〜〜〜〜〜〜〜〜〜〜〜

If you have an aversion to your child's saying the "B" sentence ("I'm bored, Mom!"), you are a prime candidate for the job of teaching him how to become responsible for his own entertainment. Don't fall into the trap of thinking that *you* have to meet the entertainment demands your child makes of you. Instead, give your child the choice between finding something to do or doing a job for you; then sit back and wait. Most children quickly decide that the rewards of using their own ingenuity to find ways to occupy their time far outweigh the costs—precisely the conclusion you were hoping your child might draw from your proposal.

PREVENTING THE PROBLEM

REDUCE THE AMOUNT OF TELEVISION-VIEWING ALLOWED. One reason children become bored so easily is that they often have unlimited access to television programs or movies to plug into their VCR's. When you limit your child's access to electronic games and television, you force him to become creative in finding things to do to entertain himself.

MODEL ANTI-BOREDOM TACTICS. When children see their parents busily engaged in enjoyable pursuits, such as reading, writing, making things, playing games, or carrying on conversations, they learn that they, too, can entertain themselves in similar ways. Shrugging your shoulders and saying, "There's nothing to do," to your spouse when

faced with a Saturday night with the children, for example, is only modeling the bored language and behavior you're trying to prevent.

SOLVING THE PROBLEM

What to Do

HELP CHILDREN LIST THINGS TO DO. When your child uses the "B" sentence, ask him to get some paper and pencil. Say, "We are going to make a list of fun things to do. One rule we will have is that whatever goes on the list must be free of charge. Now let's see how many things you can put on your list." It is important to praise the effort your child is making in the creation of the list. Once the list is finished, praise the length of the list, the variety of activities listed, and the creativity shown in making the list. This exercise shows a child how to overcome boredom in a way that is self-generated rather than parent-provided.

OFFER BORED CHILDREN CHOICES. When your child complains of being bored, offer him the choice of finding something constructive to do or of working for you. Say, "I'm sorry you have chosen to be bored. You may find something to do, or I'll find a job for you to do. You choose which option you want." (See JOB CARDS in the "Discipline Dictionary.") When given these two choices, a child will generally choose the path that gives him the greatest reward at the least cost: finding something constructive to do to occupy his time.

REWARD ANTI-BOREDOM TACTICS. When you see your child doing constructive, creative activities, praise his ability to combat boredom. Say, "How nice! You have found something to do to keep from being bored." In addition, offer to play with your child when he has spent some time finding something to do for a while. Say, "Let's see if you can play by yourself until eleven this morning, and then I will play a game with you."

WHEN ALL ELSE FAILS . . . If your child can find nothing to do except play video games or watch television, you may want to set up a token economy and allow him to earn tokens for entertaining himself creatively. He can then use the tokens to purchase television-viewing time, video-game playing time, or even complaining time. Five tokens could pay for five minutes of television-viewing, thirty tokens for thirty minutes, etcetera.

What Not to Do

DON'T RESCUE YOUR BORED CHILD. When your child complains of boredom, avoid finding something entertaining for him to do. Rescuing him from his boredom only delays his learning to entertain himself.

DON'T GET ANGRY WHEN YOUR CHILD COMPLAINS OF BOREDOM. Your anger only serves to give your child attention for the behavior you want to fade away. Instead of getting angry, encourage your child to be creative by offering the alternative of doing jobs when he says, "I'm bored."

∧∧∧∧∧∧∧∧∧∧∧∧∧∧∧∧∧∧∧∧∧∧∧∧∧

Shiftless, Listless Schifman

"That's boring!" Marty Schifman droned after every suggestion his mother made of something fun to do. Mrs. Schifman decided to figure out a plan so that her seven-year-old son would not behave like such a listless, do-nothing child all the time.

Calling Marty in the living room one morning, she began to explain the new rule. "First, we'll make a list of all the things you like to do; then we'll see if we have those things here at home. Some examples I can think of would be watching television, playing with your baseball cards, playing video games, or playing outside with your friends."

Marty only rolled his eyes in response. "Next, we'll turn index cards into job cards by listing jobs on them, such as cleaning out the flower beds or vacuuming behind the furniture. Then when you can't find something entertaining to do and say you're bored, I'll let you pick a card from this deck. Working should keep you from being so bored."

"You mean I have to work if I feel bored?" Marty chimed in.

"No, only if you can't find anything to do to keep yourself from being bored," his mother calmly explained. "You see, being bored is your choice. Only you can decide whether or not to be bored; nobody else can decide that for you.

"The last thing we'll do is make a daily schedule of the television programs you really like," Mrs. Schifman continued. "Then we'll make a rule that you can only watch one hour of television each day."

"You mean I can't watch television?" Marty asked, incredulous. "I'll really be bored! There won't be anything to do at all."

"I think television-watching is keeping you from finding something more interesting to do, so this is an experiment to see if I'm right," Mrs. Schifman replied. "Let's get started making the list of things that you enjoy doing."

So Marty and his mom made the fun activities list. They were both surprised at how many things they found right at home that he liked to do. Marty would occasionally complain about being bored, but he didn't enjoy picking a card from the job deck and having to do the job.

The words "I'm bored" began to fade from his vocabulary, much to Mrs. Schifman's pleasure. She was gratified to see how happy and creative Marty had become—he now spent time building things, reading, and creating new games to play.

Watching Too Much Television

("What's the big deal about watching television? Everybody does it!")

∧∧∧∧∧∧∧∧∧∧∧∧∧∧∧∧∧∧∧∧∧∧∧∧∧∧∧∧∧∧∧

Television-viewing is only problematic when parents don't set limits on how much, and what kind of, television programming their child is allowed to watch. The values and expectations, as well as the waistlines, of middle-years children can be placed in jeopardy if television-viewing becomes the main extracurricular activity. There are four major areas of concern around excessive TV exposure:

1. the emphasis on violence in television programming, which can desensitize young viewers to violence and aggressiveness in real life;

2. the emphasis on products in television commercials as the keys to happiness and success;

3. the tendency for children to gain weight from eating high-fat foods while being sedentary for long periods of time in front of the television, and

4. the emphasis on stereotypes that give children an unrealistic picture of relationships and emotions.

Become aware of what your child is watching when she has earned or has contracted for television-viewing time. Use the medium as a link, to enhance, not reduce, family understanding and communication.

PREVENTING THE PROBLEM

RESTRICT WEEKLY VIEWING. Your child should have definite restrictions on the number of hours of television she is allowed to watch each day. The content of the programs should also be carefully monitored so that those you find unsuitable can be eliminated from her schedule.

DEVELOP A WEEKLY TELEVISION-VIEWING SCHEDULE. In order to control the number of hours that your child spends viewing television, meet with her each week to review the television schedule for that week. Once the schedule is approved by you and your child, it should not be varied.

MODEL AND ENCOURAGE ALTERNATIVE ACTIVITIES. Parents who spend their evenings and weekends reading, conversing, or doing other creative activities model appropriate alternatives to television-viewing. Moreover, by praising your child for engaging in reading, studying, and other creative activities, you will lessen her desire to spend time in the passive pastime of television-viewing.

SOLVING THE PROBLEM

What to Do

SELL TELEVISION-VIEWING TIME. If you are faced with a vidiot, a television-viewing addict, develop a contract through which she can earn television-viewing time by working at jobs around your house. The higher the cost of television time, the less likely she will be to purchase it. Say, "When you have washed the floor in the kitchen, you may watch thirty minutes of television."

LOCK THE TELEVISION. You can lock the television so that your child cannot watch any programs when you aren't around to monitor her viewing. The most basic television lock is a lockable metal box, preferably with a clasp, so that it can be padlocked. Unplug the television and put the plug in the box. When the lid is locked, the television can't be plugged in.

ENFORCE CONSEQUENCES FOR CLANDESTINE VIEWING. If you catch your vidiot watching television when she isn't supposed to, assign her a job to do outdoors or in an area of the house where a television isn't within her viewing distance. If she sneaks back to watch television before her assigned job is completed, assign her another job. Say, "I'm sorry that you chose not to do your chore. Because you made that choice, you also chose to do another job."

ENCOURAGE YOUR CHILD TO READ. Pay your child for each book she reads to motivate her to choose reading over a more passive activity. Here's how the payment plan works: When your child finishes reading a book, take her to the bookstore and let her use that money to purchase another book.

MAKE TELEVISION-VIEWING TIME THE REWARD FOR READING. Play "let's make a deal" with your child. Say, "When you have read a book for thirty minutes, then you may watch thirty minutes of television. The shows that your child watches must be on the preapproved schedule for the week.

Note: Make sure that your child does not accrue an excessive amount of television-viewing time with this contract.

What Not to Do

DON'T NAG TELEVISION-VIEWERS TO "KICK THE HABIT." Guilt-producing techniques (such as saying, "You must be a real slob to watch so much television") are bound to backfire—your child will simply be encouraged to sneak around you to watch programs.

DON'T MAKE TELEVISION-VIEWING RULES YOU CAN'T ENFORCE. A rule that your child may not watch television while she is home alone is a rule you cannot enforce. Either let her watch television while you aren't home or lock the television.

AVOID MAKING TELEVISION-VIEWING THE CENTER OF FAMILY ACTIVITIES. Instead of using television-viewing as the most frequent form of family entertainment, set aside evenings for games, discussions, reading, crafts, and other creative activities.

Unplugging Jennifer

Jennifer Hardy was an eleven-year-old "vidiot" who would sit for hours watching what her mother considered drivel. "Jennifer, you watch that box too much!" Mrs. Hardy would complain. "Go outside and play."

Jennifer would follow her mother's orders and go out to play; but in a few minutes, she would be back in front of the television, as if drawn by some invisible force.

Realizing that Jennifer needed to be taught how much time was appropriate for television-viewing, her mother decided to impose some restrictions that she could consistently enforce.

First, she announced a new house rule that allowed only

one hour of television-viewing per day. Then she asked Jennifer to sit with her and plan the daily schedule for that hour.

At first, Jennifer stomped her foot, whining, "It's not fair! Other kids get to watch as much as they want!" Not taken in by this little display of temper, her mother simply said, "I know, dear, but it's the rule at our house that only one hour per day of television-viewing is allowed."

Jennifer tried to avoid the rule by sneaking in extra television-viewing time each day after school. When she saw what Jennifer was doing, her mother decided to alter her plan to block this new turn of events.

"Jennifer," she said, "because you want to watch more than the rule allows, I'm willing to let you watch as much as you can afford. So the new rule is: 'You may have one hour of free television-viewing each day. Every thirty minutes of viewing time after that will cost one dollar.' "

"Great!" Jennifer shouted as she ran for her piggy bank. This sounded like a simple way for her to get to watch her beloved "box," but it didn't take long for Jennifer to deplete her cash supply—it was gone in a week!

Realizing Jennifer's predicament, Mrs. Hardy offered to find her jobs to do so that she could earn money. But the jobs were hard, and Jennifer soon tired of working all the time. Besides, she realized that she couldn't watch her favorite programs when she was working!

Her mother suggested that she read, but Jennifer didn't like to read. So her mother offered to pay her one dollar for each book of over 100 pages that Jennifer read and discussed with her. With the money she received by reading, she bought more books than she had ever been able to before.

After a few weeks of reading to earn dollars, Jennifer decided that watching television was too boring and too expensive. To her mother's delight, Jennifer also concluded that creating art projects and reading, as well as playing with her friends, brightened her days more than any television screen had ever been able to do.

Index

About the Authors

∧∧∧∧∧∧∧∧∧∧∧∧∧∧∧∧∧∧∧∧∧∧∧∧∧∧∧∧∧∧

JERRY L. WYCKOFF, PH.D., is a family therapist who specializes in parent-child relationships and child management. Co-author of *Discipline Without Shouting or Spanking*, Dr. Wyckoff is currently assistant professor of human development at Ottawa University (Kansas) and is also in private practice.

BARBARA C. UNELL is the co-founder and editor of *Twins* magazine, the host of a daily parenting information feature on the Associated Press Radio Network, and the co-author of *Discipline Without Shouting or Spanking* and *Anorexia Nervosa: Finding the Lifeline*, as well as the author of numerous books about relationships and family life.